FIRE

of

HOPE

FINDING TREASURE
IN THE RUBBLE

by

SHAUNA L. HOEY

Praise for Fire of Hope

"*Fire of Hope* is a necessary book, a masterful, step-by-step guide on the journey from tragedy to healing. In it, Shauna Hoey bridges the clinical effects of trauma and loss with the language of the heart, mind, soul, and spirit. If you have experienced trauma or loss, *Fire of Hope* will benefit you."
—Christie Lee, MA, MFT, LPC, AAMFT

"*Fire of Hope* captures the fearful spirit of the trauma surrounding the days of the Waldo Canyon fire, along with the faithful spirit that brought a community of caring people together. Shauna Hoey brings lessons in courage and commitment in turning her personal burdens into blessings for others!"
—Rev. David L. Hunting
Retired Pastor of First Congregational Church
Public Information Officer of Manitou Springs Fire Dept.

"As I read, I kept thinking of people I know who need to read this book now. There is nothing like it out there. This book helps fire and trauma victims, counselors, first responders, concerned friends and families of those in any crisis."
—Elizabeth S. LeMarr

"Shauna's book is full of heart-felt stories of the tears, healing, and triumph over life's darkest moments."
—Jennifer Darling, author of
Amazon best seller *Discover Your Inspiration*

Praise for Fire of Hope

"I was deeply moved and felt as if I had entered this very personal and communal tragedy in a new and different way."

—M. R. Hyde

"Loved it! Shauna tells a beautiful, heartbreaking, heart-healing tale of her journey from her point of view of losing her home in the Waldo Canyon fire. I was so moved by the vulnerability and the personal stories of other fire victims. Having lost my home, too, I found myself crying and nodding my head throughout, feeling validated, but also encouraged.

Shauna sheds light on areas I didn't understand, like how trauma that isn't totally dealt with can resurface. The tools and ideas she provides to aid in the process are very practical, and I know I'll be drawing on this wisdom myself. Very well done and healing!"

—Holly DeHerrera

"True, *Fire of Hope* is fascinating Colorado history. But even more, it is therapy for those who have suffered real trauma from loss—be it by fire, accident, or any other tragedy such as the death of a loved one. Read this memoir-like account and gain psychological insights that will stick with you forever, even as you wipe the tears from your eyes."

—Greg Austin, author
First Passion

ISBN 978-1-943650-55-2
Library of Congress Control Number 2017942318
Editing by Bonnie McDermid, Wordsmith.Ink
Cover design by Julie Campbell, Camven Media
   and Holy Moly Studios
Author photo on back cover by Johnny Wilson

Printed in the United States of America

Published by Thrive With Hope Publishing, Manitou Springs, CO

Visit www.ThriveWithHope.com

Thrive With Hope

Dedication

To the survivors who rebuilt their lives
and to those who are making a safe haven
for their hearts and homes.
May you find the light and love you need
to make your way out of the valley of darkness.

*Even though I walk through the darkest valley,
I will fear no evil, for you are with me;
your rod and your staff, they comfort me.*

Psalm 23:4
New International Version

Table of Contents

Section Three—Rebuilding

Section Four—Gifts From the Ashes

Preface

I'M NOT A COUNSELOR OR A SOCIAL WORKER, but an ordinary person who lived through a life-changing, traumatic event. My hope is to share resources so that others can recover, too.

When I started this book, I didn't intend to share my own story, only those of others, because I thought their stories were more significant. Others had lost much more than I and I felt ashamed of my grief.

In time, however, I came to understand that each person's account, including my own, represents a changed life and deserves a voice. I went to great lengths to preserve and safeguard each story with accuracy, sensitivity, and approval from each person. Any errors are mine.

The weight of trauma is heavy. The powerful effects of natural disasters on people often take years to recover from. Financial ruin caused by a lack of resources, insurance battles, and health-related ailments negatively affects peoples' lives for the long term.

Yet, I wanted to write a book that would feel light in the hands of my readers.

This book cannot fully represent all of the experiences people go through after a natural disaster, especially the stories of those who have lost loved ones. I acknowledge the heartache of many people not represented in my book.

Fire of Hope focuses on the people displaced by the Waldo Canyon fire. The Black Forest fire, which struck our community less than a year later, is only spoken about in my book by one family. However, many of the lessons and much of the hope gleaned from these stories can be applied to any disaster.

If, after a great trauma, you have not yet reestablished your own refuge of security and stability or a place to call home, I hope you find comfort through the pages of this book.

Acknowledgements

A HEARTFELT THANK YOU goes to Johnny Wilson for listening to my story with ears that cared, eyes that saw with deepest compassion, and a heart full of love for others. Johnny inspired me to tell my story and the stories of others.

I am grateful to the people who shared their stories with transparency so that others may find hope. The contributors to my book are the healers in our communities, because of their willingness to embrace others with their experience, strength, and hope. They have filled me with love and friendship.

My husband, Rex, and my children, Andrea and Caleb, deserve my warmest thanks for their generous support, prayers, and patience while I spent endless hours on my computer. I am blessed to have a family that supports my dreams. I am grateful for my stepdaughter, Jillian, who inspired me and led by example.

I thank my writing coach, Larry J. Leech II, with my deepest gratitude for smoothing my writing flaws with his patience, skill, and nurturing spirit. Thank you, Larry, for drawing out my transparent story and my writing voice.

I acknowledge with great thankfulness the following people who supported me. My mom, Karen Frank, loves and supports me with endless encouragement: I'm thankful for her eagle-eyed editing and honest feedback.

Sue LeMarr fueled my spirit and gave me insight into my early drafts: I'm thankful for her encouragement and inspiration.

Penny and Francis Narain believed in me and shared my excitement about my project.

Acknowledgements

Jean Bessey supported me with endless encouragement and faithful friendship.

Authors and friends, Holly DeHerrera and M. R. Hyde, shared their time and talent to review my book.

Thank you Laura McBee and Marie Turner and Sue LeMarr for your valuable feedback as first readers.

My editors, Greg Austin and Bonnie McDermid, guided me with patience and excellence in their craft and they have been a joy to work with.

Aaron Zook and Sarah Sullivan proofread my book.

Michelle Tennesen led me to dream about possibilities.

Liz Cobb shared her experience with the interview process.

My marketing director, Beverly Banks, inspired and led me with her expertise.

Jen Darling supported me with her talent and incredible skill set.

Finally, I'm grateful to my Lord who blessed me with the precious people in my life who gave me strength and loved me through tough times.

Introduction

THE 2012 WALDO CANYON FIRE OF COLORADO burned 347 homes becoming, at that time, the most destructive in the state's history in loss of structures.[1] My house was one of them. Although I wasn't living in it at the time of the fire, the effects of trauma affected me as if I had been.

The fire ravaged our neighborhoods and stripped our mountains. During a seventeen-day span, 18,247[2] acres burned. Two people died. Thanks to committed first responders and compliant citizens, everyone else escaped without injury. More than 32,000 citizens evacuated from over a dozen mountain communities. Depending on the area, the fire displaced families from their homes for days, weeks, even months.

Less than a year later, when we were about to commemorate the first anniversary of the Waldo Canyon fire, another fire struck our Colorado Springs community. The Black Forest fire then became the most destructive fire in loss of structures in Colorado history, destroying 486 homes and 14,000 acres of ponderosa pine forest. Two more people died in that fire.[3]

If a traumatic event has affected you or someone you love, you are not alone. *Fire of Hope: Finding Treasure in the Rubble* peers into my own life and the lives of people who lived through the devastation caused by fire.

Many of us struggled to understand the effects of trauma. We questioned ourselves because we didn't know what was normal. For most of us, moving past our grief caused more stress than we expected. Some people took longer to begin the healing process. Others got stuck. I met people who, paralyzed by heartache, were unable to move forward.

Through a difficult process, I found ways to heal and became determined to support others traumatized by a natural disaster.

And I chose to write the book I couldn't find when I needed answers.

The material here is relevant for those who need to work through the effects of loss caused by natural disasters and other traumas. I have attempted to provide keys you can use to heal and insights to help you support loved ones.

In this book, you will become acquainted with the people I interviewed and with whom I shared experiences. You will follow our stories through each chapter—my narrative first, followed by each person's story.

Our accounts share what we experienced and how we coped. We survived disaster and worked to recover. We invite you into the events that broke our hearts and changed our lives.

Welcome to our stories of hope.

Section One

Devastation Devours

Chapter 1

My View From the Ashes

*Brokenness summons light into
the deepest crevices of our hearts.*

I STOOD ON MY COLLAPSED GARAGE DOOR, stunned by the devastation. Tangled in emotions, I could only stare at the ruins of my home—now a pit of ashes mixed with shards of broken memories.

Until that moment, I never realized how much I depend on structure, predictable routines, and the place I call *home*. I drive to work and expect the school to be standing when I pull into the parking lot.

Photo by Laura McCracken

After a long day, I expect to unlock the door to my home, throw my purse and keys on the kitchen table, hear the voices of my children, and feel my husband's embrace.

But overnight, my home and my neighborhood had burned to the ground. Life as I knew it was smoking rubble.

What I would soon learn was that, even if our lives turn to rubble, we don't have to stay in the debris. Our brokenness summons light into the deepest crevices of our hearts. And at that point, we have a choice to crumple in a heap of defeat or refocus our lives.

I chose the latter.

Although the doors of my home were burnt, the doors in my heart were opened. The fire turned my well-ordered life raw side out, leaving me vulnerable, my tears erupting like lava from a volcano. Its heat melted my self-sufficiency and withered my pride, making room for new relationships.

Fire stripped away the clutter in my life. It taught me to cherish what matters and to not waste time on the unimportant. Looking back, I see that I am fragile—and so is everything I hold dear. Now, I don't take my precious days for granted.

I recall the day the fire started like it was yesterday.

Chapter 2

Packing to Evacuate

I FIRST NOTICED THE STRANGE-LOOKING PLUME of smoke when I was still seventy miles south of my home in Manitou Springs, Colorado. Caleb, my 11-year-old son, and I were driving back from New Mexico on Interstate 25 on that Saturday afternoon. We were eager to get home and pack so he could leave for Eagle Lake summer camp the next day.

The cloud seemed to grow larger with each passing mile, along with my alarm. By the time I took the Manitou Springs exit, I could see smoke billowing over the mountaintop; it appeared to be uncomfortably close to our house.

My heart pounding, I called Rex, my husband, and asked if he knew what was happening. A few minutes later, he met us in the driveway and quickly told us about the wildfire. From our front yard, we could see that the fire was, in fact, less than three miles away, just beyond the next neighborhood.

Thus, on June 23, 2012, the Waldo Canyon fire began. It would eventually torch 347 homes, kill two people, destroy 18,247 acres, and take seventeen days to contain.

Based on the proximity of the flames and on news reports, Rex, Caleb, and I had time to pack—unlike the people higher on the mountain. We calculated that the fire would have to move down the mountain and burn through two miles of houses before it reached us, so we kept an eagle eye on the smoke and flames while we gathered our belongings.

Cedar Heights and Garden of the Gods, which were less than two miles away, had already been evacuated. Caleb's camp was not only evacuated, but closed. People from over a dozen mountain communities within fifteen to twenty miles of Colorado Springs would have to flee to refuge in dread and desperation. Over the next week, evacuations would increase to nearly 32,000 people.

As I swept through the house, my thoughts and feelings vacillated between denial and reality. I felt like I was watching myself acting in a bad sci-fi movie. *My house will be fine, so whatever I put in the car will have to be unloaded and put away again.* At the same time, I could see that our house might, indeed, burn.

Caleb shadowed me. Any panic on my part would have scared him, so I remained calm. He followed my instructions and together we packed.

Rex packed the upstairs office while Caleb and I hurried downstairs. The first items on my mind were our photo albums. I had spent years crafting scrapbooks to capture my babies' childhood—we even had bookshelves custom-built to hold my albums full of those artistically arranged photos. Remaking the albums would be impossible, so we earnestly packed and brought them to our one-car garage.

Next, I took down our irreplaceable family photos from the wall. Caleb helped me wrap them in towels and together we carefully stacked them in the car.

Outside, the firestorm seemed to be generating its own weather system of hot, swirling winds. Inside, the heat was suffocating because our 1954-vintage home wasn't built with air conditioning. Accustomed to cool mountain breezes, we struggled in temperatures over 100 degrees.

Moving upstairs, Caleb made short work of packing for his thirteen-year-old sister, Andrea, who was still in Albuquerque.

He had called her and was rushing around her bedroom collecting her favorite clothes, gymnastics medals, and photos. Hearing them talk on the speakerphone and watching Caleb calmly pack her stuff brought order to a chaotic scene. The history of their loving relationship gave me solid ground to stand on at that time of uncertainty.

Caleb loaded Andrea's bag into my car and then turned his attention to his own things. "Mom, what should I pack?" I hurried to his room and we decided on his wrestling medals, a bunny picture from a special friend, some clothes.

Rex's Honda Accord was already loaded with our computer, its back-up drive, and important documents. He had started working in the steaming hot attic where Caleb and I quickly joined him. Rex dripped with sweat as he carried boxes down the ladder and out to his scorching car. Every time he re-entered our house, I could feel the heat radiate from his clothes.

Outside, the air hummed with chatter and the sounds of organized chaos not far away. I walked over to my next-door neighbor's house to check on them. They continued loading their truck while we talked.

"This is unreal!" I said.

Paige threw up her arms, exasperated, "Really!"

Eyes locked, reflecting the same emotions. Having a moment to speak reminded each of us that we were in this together.

People in my neighborhood protect each other. We live with our homes snuggled close together, blessed with mountain views and old-town charm. Most of our homes had been built one at a time between the '50s and '70s. The beauty of our houses is matched only by our mutual concern for each other.

Suddenly, we realized that our neighbor across the street was out of town. We called her cell phone and explained the pre-evacuation alert. She told us where to find her spare key and important documents. Entering her personal space was awkward, but necessary. We gathered her choice belongings and then continued our own packing.

I called my mom, a retired insurance agent. She told me to take photos of everything. "Open every cupboard and every drawer and take photos. Don't forget the garage and shed." I rushed through the inside and around the outside of our house, snapping photos.

After that first round of work, I took a moment to breathe. *Isn't it strange that my car is half-full and I have all I need?*

Rested somewhat and able to face the draining heat again, I went through the house a second time. In spite of the fire stalking our neighborhood, this time I was going to be more selective.

And suddenly, I remembered the journals I had written for my kids, two for each of them. They were especially precious because they held my written memories of their childhood, a time that couldn't be recaptured.

I knelt to open the cedar chest at the foot of our bed; the lid creaked open. Sifting anxiously through the memorabilia, I started to panic. I couldn't see the journals.

But then... *Yes, there they are!* I gripped the books tightly to my chest, gasping at the thought of ever losing them.

Next, I hurried through my jewelry chest and found treasures I had nearly missed. First, a small box covered with a tattered ribbon and random globs of scotch tape. My four-year-old son had wrapped my gift after Papa had taken him Christmas shopping. I pulled out the beat-up watch— I had worn it until the leather band faded and fell apart—all because of the heart of a little boy for his mama. Tears dripped as I held the box decorated with so much love and looked at the worn-out watch I treasured.

Then, my grandmother's silver whistle caught my eye. I snatched it up, remembering she had carried it for thirty-five years as a middle school teacher. (In 1955, Grandma had been the first in our family to graduate from college.) When I started my first teaching job, she gifted me her whistle. I rubbed my fingers over the engraving. Grandma's initials were on one side, T.E.A. 1953, and my initials, S.L.E. 1993, on the other. This was another treasure that would have burned if....

Remembering I had another stash of old photo negatives and pictures (organized, but never placed in an album), I knelt and gathered them from under the bed. They could have been lost forever.

It took but a moment or two to secure them in the car. Then I rested, taking a moment to sit and breathe. I felt relieved.

The third round of searching, however, was the most painful. Mindful of the treasures I had just rescued, I wiped my sweaty brow and knelt to look under our bed again. Carefully tucked in the corner was the tin lockbox from my deceased grandparents.

I am the family historian—the keeper of the family birth certificates and records from over a hundred years ago. Again I gasped at how close I had come to losing them, as there were no copies stored anywhere else.

"The letters—oh, no!—the love letters from WWII!" I quickly untied the string-wrapped packet and opened one.

My Darling, please take me along in your heart.
For you and I are one, My Darling. You are my life.

I folded the letter and placed it back in the envelope. These were the love letters written by my grandparents to each other during the war. They were married sixty-seven years before death separated them.

I stood to riffle through the bedroom closet, searching for the hand-beaded purse I carried at my wedding. My godmother had made it for me, stitching many hours of love into a beautiful gift. I found it next to a collection of clay figurines made by our children.

How could I have left these things? I clutched them to my chest and thought, *Home is the place where the ills of the world shouldn't touch me. I should be able to control who and what enters here, ensuring it is a place of refuge and comfort for my family.*

The fire was undeniably threatening my safe place—my home.

The sudden beat of helicopters overhead—like an alarm warning us of impending danger—made my stomach churn. I rushed outside. The choppers and the smoke ambushed my senses. I felt like a lost child, not knowing which way to turn.

Above me, choppers carried huge water buckets that swayed to and fro at the end of long cables. Those flying workhorses disappeared into the smoke and then emerged after dumping each load, flying away again to refill at our local reservoirs. Other choppers dropped fire retardant, spreading the chemical over the blaze like a red rooster tail.

During the whole next week, that incessant beat of the choppers would fade in and out, around the clock. In time, their sound comforted me because those firefighters stood between me, my family, my house, and the fire.

We worried for others as well as for ourselves. Crystal Park, a gated community just one mile up the mountain from our neighborhood, was evacuating early. And the only way down was a single steep, narrow, winding road. Beginning early in the morning, a constant stream of loaded SUVs—some pulling overloaded trailers—clunked down that road. Pets stuck their heads out the windows with their tongues hanging out.

Several hours later, eerie silence descended on our neighborhood. There was no more traffic because the Crystal Park evacuation was complete. We learned that our neighborhood would be the last to evacuate from Manitou Springs.

I stood in our front yard, warily eyeing the smoke. Up on the mountain, dry evergreens and oaks made mini-explosions as they burst into flame. And suddenly, the red monster flared up, the smoke swelling into a massive black billow. Erratic winds were shifting the fire. We weren't sure, but it seemed like it was moving away from us.

"Oh, my God," I cried out, and yelled for my husband.

Our neighbors climbed up onto their roof to get a better view as we kept watch from our front yard.

Our cars were packed and ready to leave at a moment's notice. But instead of leaving, we waited. We knew that if we left, the roads would be blocked and we would be unable to return. Emergency cell lines would be jammed, local hotels filled. We wanted to stay until evacuation was mandatory.

That night, the horribly toxic air forced us to close our windows. Every breath filled our noses with an acidy, burnt-toast kind of smell. I kept opening a window, hoping for at least one breath of fresh air, but each time the smoky air burned my lungs. I had to shut the window and endure our sweat box.

Our evacuation order came the next morning when Emergency Services called. We chose not to leave. Some of our neighbors also decided to stay. Many of our neighbors lived in the homes their families had owned for generations. They felt that, by staying, they could protect their homes and family history.

We told ourselves we would leave if the fire progressed too far in our direction. We had a clear view of the blazing monster and knew we could get out in a hurry. The fire would have to jump a two-lane freeway and burn through dozens of houses before it came to our street.

We continually monitored the situation. We were holding tight.

Had I known then what I know now, I would have left.

In the morning, the fire shifted away again, forcing other communities to evacuate. Our firefighters had been able to contain the fire with the help of the wind, and it was no longer an immediate threat to Manitou Springs. Authorities removed the mandatory evacuation in our neighborhood.

But bad news lurked in the smoky shadows, waiting to explode my world.

Chapter 3

What Remained

WITH MY FAMILY SAFE and our Manitou Springs home seemingly secure for the time being, my focus turned to our rental property in Mountain Shadows, eight miles away.

My children and I had lived in the yellow house when I was a single mom after a divorce. That home meant far more to me than people realized, and its destruction was the catalyst for profound healing in my life.

I had experienced many losses in my youth that cost me the people I loved and structure I depended on. My parents divorced when I was five. Subsequent marriages and divorces multiplied the losses, the emotional scars, and the deep need for a place to call my own.

That yellow house was mine—a refuge that couldn't be taken from me, an environment over which I had control. Not only was it mine, it was beautiful and safe, a peaceful haven from my past losses and a special place for a new beginning. Little did I know that my home—a symbol of safety—would soon raise buried memories I had put to rest.

My children were two and three when I bought the house. Like a favorite chapter from a treasured storybook, our years living there were close to my heart. Memories from those pages flooded me. I remember pulling Andrea and Caleb around the neighborhood in our red wagon. Caleb always took his bouncy ball along, while Andrea brought her stuffed animals and our pet rabbit, Little Gray. She would push Little Gray around the neighborhood in her doll stroller. And when he tried to escape, she scolded him and stuffed him back into her stroller.

On nice, warm days, Andrea and Caleb would slide down the Slip 'N Slide on the hill in our backyard. In the winter, they would slide down the same hill on their snow saucers. I would smile, watching them in their puffed-up snowsuits, pink faces peeking out. Afterward, we always defrosted in the kitchen with cups of hot chocolate, the space heater by our feet.

The best memory was being happy and safe in our lovely home, winter and summer.

Before buying the yellow house, we had lived in Albuquerque, New Mexico. When my ex-husband, David, was reassigned to the Air Force base in Colorado Springs, the children and I followed him so they could remain close to their dad.

Everything we needed to move and live in Colorado Springs had fallen perfectly into place; I found a teaching job and a house, all within a week.

The realtor brought me to the yellow house. As I pushed open the front door and stepped inside, sunlight beamed through giant picture windows and mountains with a bright blue backdrop filled my senses. The cottage charm stole my heart. Instantly, I knew this was my house.

Even before stepping into the living room I said, "Let's make an offer." We wrote my offer for more than the asking price. Two other buyers made offers that same day—for cash. Mine was based on a mortgage. I held my breath until I got the call from my realtor, "You got the house!" "Yes!" I did a happy dance.

I met Rex that same year and married him almost two years later. After our wedding, we moved into Rex's house in Manitou Springs, which had more room for our combined family, and rented out the yellow house.

Losing my balance, I fell over the walkway step in our front yard. Pain burned my knees and, though stunned, I refocused on the sky. Days after the fire started, flames still raged 150 feet above the treetops. It looked like fire had engulfed the whole mountain and colored the entire sky with an eerie red glow.

Staring up at the high, smoky billows, I got to my feet, bits of ash floating around me, and brushed the flakes off my arms and legs. Time to get back to work—I had to handle everything alone now because Rex, an airline pilot, had left for Europe two days after the fire began.

I searched for news about the neighborhoods affected by the fire and hoped the yellow house was safe. News reports relieved me for the moment.

By Day Four of the Waldo Canyon fire, the Mountain Shadows neighborhood around our yellow house had been evacuated. At one point, the winds shifted away and residents were allowed to return to their homes for thirty minutes (with police escort). Glad for a reprieve from the constant threat, many families returned, but the winds proved erratic and suddenly shifted the fire toward Mountain Shadows again. As fire sprouted on the hillsides above their homes, folks had to flee their neighborhoods once more.

The 5:00 p.m. news reported the first structures burning on Flying W Ranch Road, which ran behind my yellow house.

Someone posted on Twitter, "OH DEAR GOD...this is terrifying!"

My mind spun; our house might, indeed, burn. I tried to find ground to stand on that didn't feel like quicksand. Desperately, I searched the Internet for information about the affected areas, but couldn't find the answers I needed. The media wouldn't give out street names so I couldn't figure out which neighborhoods were on fire. I watched all the news updates, but they couldn't keep up with the fast-moving inferno. It made me realize how dependent we were on media coverage in a crisis.

I called the company that managed our property and asked if they had information about our house. They didn't. I sat with my head in my hands wondering if our yellow house was as good as gone.

The fire monster continued to spread, driven by sixty-five mile-per-hour winds. Public Health issued a warning about unhealthy air quality. I watched the smoke from our front yard and stayed glued to the news. I was exhausted from the stress. What would happen next? Would the fire turn toward us again? How long would this fire rage without containment? Our beloved mountains were burning and hundreds of homes were already gone.

Some of our Manitou Springs neighbors began to return. But I wasn't ready to unpack my car in case the fire shifted toward us again. We needed to stay on guard.

The severe heat concerned me. Our cars heated to over 120 degrees when they sat in the sun. I didn't want my photos and computer drive to melt like my neighbor's had. They had packed the backup drive for their family business in their truck, but the heat warped the drive and destroyed it. In their effort to protect their business records, they lost them.

***

Could there ever be a good way to find out your house has burned down? I'll never forget Day Six of the fire. I was standing alone in the kitchen when the phone rang and the property manager spoke. He had found an aerial photograph of the Mountain Shadows area.

"Your house is gone."

The words stabbed deeply, yet I responded calmly and thanked him for letting me know, as if it had been an ordinary phone call. But why did I act *normal* on hearing such terrible news? I hung up, trying to process his cold words. Then I collapsed, face to the ground, knees to my heart, hands clenched—I sobbed until I could finally stand again.

Stunned, I didn't remember anything for the next several hours.

That evening, a formal meeting was held at the University of Colorado, Colorado Springs (UCCS) to inform residents of the condition of their homes. Even though the property manager had told me my house hadn't survived, I attempted denial. *Officials could have made a mistake. The property manager could have been wrong. Our home might have been spared.* Other people had also been told their homes were gone, based on aerial photos. But like me, they still held out hope.

We all gathered to support each other and to get final confirmation, one way or the other. Surprisingly, the impersonal gym felt warm with people who cared. We waited an hour before officials ushered us into smaller rooms organized by neighborhoods.

I looked for our tenants, Bill and Elaine, but couldn't find them. I had called them, but they hadn't responded.

The waiting continued in the smaller rooms. I sat at a round table with a group of people I didn't know. We hoped for good news with our chins up and our eyes fixed on each other. I would rather have bad news than none at all; not knowing kept me churning with anxiety. In some ways, the waiting may have been the worst part of the fire—dealing with the constant, unsettled feelings, wondering whether our homes had been destroyed.

Finally, the meeting leaders began to pass out stapled packets, each a multi-page list of home addresses with DAMAGED or DESTROYED typed in bold print next to the addresses. Couldn't they have simply posted the addresses on a big screen? Even waiting for the packets to be distributed was excruciating. When all of the packets had been passed out, two tables near the back had been forgotten. I imagined how I would have felt if I were them. When they finally got their lists, I could exhale, not realizing I had been holding my breath.

I held my own packet in my hands, the cool, white paper weighing my hands down as if it were a pallet of bricks. I opened and read, my hands seeming to burn as my brain slowly registered the catastrophic losses recorded. Pages of addresses representing families whose lives would never be the same, line after endless line of addresses next to the words DAMAGED or DESTROYED. Mere ink on a page revealed many families' dire fate. I ran my fingers over the entire list, as if by touching each address I could impart my compassion.

My eyes stopped on the first letter of my street. I ran my hand down the page until I saw 2557 Hot Springs Court. Boldly printed there…DESTROYED.

I went numb. And based on the blank stares and frozen figures surrounding me, so did everyone else. I expected to hear sobs from across the room but heard nothing. I expected shoulders to slump, heads to bow, but none of that happened. Those of us at my table could find no way to express our grief. We all stared blankly, our hearts so heavy we could do nothing else.

My eyes focused on the only person at our table whose address read DAMAGED. He shared with us his hope that some of his possessions might be unharmed. I locked my eyes on him because the pain from all the others in the room threatened to overwhelm me. Looking into his eyes lightened the weight of my sadness. And I felt relieved for him because his wife had died the previous year. He could have lost all of his tangible memories of her.

The air felt thick—a fog of infirmity. Silence prevailed throughout the room.

Then the silence was broken by questions, some of them angry. After all this waiting, we were told we couldn't return to our homes due to safety concerns. More waiting.

That evening, Bill called to reassure me. The sound of his voice comforted me. He and Elaine and their two cats were safe. They hadn't received my message at first, but now we were both relieved to connect.

Later that night, I curled into a little ball and scrolled through my rapid thoughts. *What should I do first? Who should I call?*

Though still under stress, I moved into my mode of taking care of responsibilities. Providing structure and organization for others is what I do as a teacher, as a mom of two and a stepmother of four. I'm the take-charge, take-care-of-business type of person who gets the job done, so I focused my energy on people who had lost more than I and did my best to ignore my own pain.

The counselor from the school where I taught called and scheduled a meeting to support me. But because I couldn't recognize my great need for support, I conveyed to her, my co-workers, and friends I didn't need anything and urged them to give their help to people with real needs.

By the time I fell apart, people had stopped asking me about the fire. They didn't know I needed them because I had told them I was fine.

Five days after my yellow house burned, we were allowed to view the remains of our homes.

That was the day I lost it.

Chapter 4

The Day I Lost It

WE HAD TO WAIT AGAIN—for three long days after the UCCS meeting.

At last, we were allowed into the guarded area where our homes had stood. It had taken several days for the rubble to cool and for the fire department to clear the area to assure our safety.

Since the start of the fire, our police had been doing a fine job of protecting our property from scavenging thieves and our privacy from curious onlookers. They had blocked the entrances to streets affected by the fire—we even had to show proof of residency before we were allowed to enter. Each time I drove up to officers guarding the entrance, I felt so honored and thankful they were there to protect what remained.

Rex was still working out of the country. My extended family lived out of state and my children were out of town. It was all up to me. I felt numb and alone, but it wasn't smart to go by myself.

The first two friends I called couldn't come with me, so I called Laura, my friend from work, and she offered her immediate support. We decided to meet at our favorite coffee shop before entering my ravaged neighborhood.

That morning, I stood at the Starbucks counter, about to order. Mid-sentence, I froze. I tried to speak but nothing came out, as if someone was choking me.

Suddenly, my emotions erupted. I sobbed, wailed, doubled over, and in general made a lot of noise. The whole place grew quiet with concern for the wailing woman. I never did finish placing that Starbucks order.

I went outside so I wouldn't disturb the customers any more. Still wailing and sobbing beyond control, I sat in a chair, doubled over with my face in my lap. Some sweet soul drew near and asked me if I was okay.

"NO, I'M NOT OKAY!" I screamed at the top of my lungs.

Quickly, a compassionate group of ladies corralled me and prayed. A stranger cradled me in her arms, not knowing the reason for my tears, because my emotions kept sucking the words out of me. A firefighter approached asking if I might want to come to the station with him for support.

Apparently, I'd already drawn quite a crowd of support.

I'd begun to regain a bit of composure when Laura arrived on the crowded scene. She had no idea I was the person who was surrounded by the crowd, and thought someone had had a stroke or fainted.

After I stopped crying and was sitting with Laura, a reporter approached us from one of the national news networks. I explained what had happened, agreed to be interviewed, then met with her camera crew. Later that evening, my story ended up on the national news. Talking to the reporters took my mind off my emotions.

Reporters weren't allowed in the burned neighborhood, so Laura and I took their camera and shot some footage for them. Having a job to do lifted me into my take-care-of-business mode, a safe place away from my pain.

It was time to face it—I drove us into my neighborhood. What I saw shocked me, my gasps inadequate for the tragedy. The once-beautiful community looked like a scene from an apocalyptic movie. From every angle, black and gray devastation overwhelmed my senses.

A burned car on my right stunned me—all that remained was a melted frame. Charred skeletons of trees and mounds of rubble surrounded us.

Random houses still stood—spared by nature, rescued by fire fighters—tokens among the devastated homes. The ghosts of all those burned houses disoriented me at first.

Traffic signs had melted and familiar landmarks had burned. "That's my street!" I screamed, surprised to recognize it. I turned in and my heart dropped to my stomach. When I approached my cul-de-sac, I had to count driveways to find my home. Our yellow house with the white trim was now a dark heap of rubble. The new garage door had crumpled like an accordion. I got out of the car, staring silently. Then I walked up to the concrete foundation and hung my toes over the edge. I leaned forward and peered down into that pit of destruction.

The washer and dryer from the third floor now lay in the hole where the basement used to be. Record-breaking heat had bent the eight-inch structural steel beams. Nails that had held the frame together were scattered all over the property. My new fire-resistant siding had melted into cardboard-like chunks.

Broken glass and pottery crunched beneath my feet as I walked through the rubble. I noticed pieces of china with hand-painted roses and scavenged to find any dishes that might have survived whole. I was startled when a chunk of pottery burned my hand. Six days had passed since the inferno had ravaged our neighborhood. Feeling its heat made the fire feel like it was still alive—and still had power to destroy.

I looked beyond the charred mountain range—blue sky and puffy white clouds hung in stark contrast to the black and gray ash all around me. Color didn't fit with this doomsday scene. The sky should have been dark, like my countenance.

Birds sang as if nothing had happened.

I walked with Laura into the surrounding neighborhood and saw the heartbreaking sight of homeowners digging through fragments in the ashes. Some sat in the middle of their broken concrete and melted frames, head in hands. Some embraced. Others huddled on the street.

As we walked, I remembered the wild animals that had delighted my children and me when we lived here. We enjoyed watching the deer nibbling on the grass. Chasing the rabbits around the yard was one of Andrea and Caleb's favorite pastimes. The furry creatures always escaped, pursued by my children's giggles. So when I spotted a rabbit sitting on the broken concrete remains of my neighbor's house amidst the destruction, it symbolized hope and life. The video Laura and I took of the rabbit aired on the national news that same evening.

A month later, I learned that the lady who owned that house had lost her husband in combat two years before the fire, suddenly becoming a widow with two young boys. She hadn't had the strength to return to her burned home. When I told her about the nose-twitching rabbit that had given me hope, she said she felt encouraged to know the place of her great sadness was a place of refuge for the bunny.

A few days later, after Rex returned home from Europe, he saw our ruined neighborhood for the first time. I had made several trips to the sad scene while he was away and had already processed many of my emotions, so I focused my attention on him.

We pulled into our driveway and got out of the car. Rex began to walk around the property, surveying the destruction, his face solemn. Each footstep echoed against the heavy silence, broken glass from the shattered windows of our ruined house crackling under his feet. His shoulders slumped, plainly weighed down by the desolation.

"I've seen this before," he said finally. "When I was seventeen,

I had the same dream for several years—this is the place in my dream. I came here and picked up a girl crumpled in despair and carried her out of the devastation."

"Why did you pick her up?" I asked.

"She was alone and needed help."

That girl was me. Both Rex and I knew it.

The next day, we wore boots and gloves so we could search through the ashes for anything of value that might have survived. We walked with care, trying not to disturb any of Bill and Elaine's belongings that might break under our weight.

Nails and broken china were everywhere. From under several layers of debris, I pulled out a perfect, small pitcher. I later discovered it was a piece of the china set from Elaine's mother. I also found a sea green ceramic bear Elaine's daughter had given her as a gift. Both were special items that meant a lot to Elaine.

The second and third floors had collapsed into the basement, about eight feet underground. The huge pit was filled six feet deep in places with debris—broken glass, nails, jagged metal edges. Curious, Rex lowered himself into the hole to assess the situation. After he made sure nothing would hurt me, he helped me down into the basement where we continued to hunt for salvageable items.

By the time we were ready to leave, we had stacked a pile of artifacts in the driveway. The following week, I made several more trips to allow the shock of it all to soak in.

Days after my visit to the yellow house with Rex, our insurance agent met with me at our Manitou Springs house. As Rex was away at work, I had to handle the stress alone. I hadn't realized how difficult that meeting would be until the agent laid out his papers on the table and started asking me questions.

He asked me to recount every detail about the lost structure. *But the photos I had taken were of our Manitou Springs home, not the destroyed yellow house. You've got to be kidding me!*

Walking through each room in my mind triggered vivid pictures of what I had lost. What flooring was in the entry? What type of baseboards, light fixtures, and faucets in each sink? How big were the closets and how many shelves in each? Drapes or blinds? What kind? Together, we reconstructed details. From my descriptions, the agent drew a blueprint-type map and added notes.

This task required bravery beyond my ordinary supply. I pressed through each question robotically—striving hard to think logically—while a deep well of emotion boiled under each word, each memory. My house had not been just the sum of its parts. Talking about it that way truly nauseated me.

I'm surprised I made it through that exercise, which took several hours. Remembering each room, every detail, drained me. The agent put up with my scattered thinking and dribbles of tears and I had to apologize for losing my composure a couple of times. He was clearly trained for this type of crisis and guided me with patience every step of the way.

At the end of it all, I just wanted my house back. The loss felt like a gaping hole in my chest. The pain of others who had also lost their homes weighed on my heart.

My way of taking control was to do something to encourage these broken people. I hoped that if I rebuilt our house, maybe others would be inspired to do the same. Seeing a foundation being poured and a house frame springing up out of the desolation might give others the courage to rebuild, too. I planned on our house being one of the first to emerge from the wounded neighborhood.

A few days after my insurance meeting, I received a sizable

check from the insurance company. It provided me a way to resurrect my house and give hope to others. Sadly, many families were not as fortunate as Rex and I were in dealing with their insurance companies.

With most of the insurance details behind us, we moved forward. A week after we received the check, we met with a builder. Scott had been Rex's classmate at the Air Force Academy. We felt comfortable working with him because of his military background and long-time relationship with Rex.

We used the archived blueprints of the original house, retrieved from the City of Colorado Springs. I was determined to have my house back to fill the unbearable void. Focusing on the rebuild gave me a vision for the future.

When I launched into rebuilding my lost home, I had no idea I would also be rebuilding places in myself that needed healing. The debris and ashes of my yellow house symbolized the ashes from other losses in my life that still needed care. I had a choice between accepting this time of grief as an opportunity to grow or as a tragedy that would haunt me for the rest of my life. I chose growth and healing.

I resolved that I wouldn't allow one tear or one moment of heartache to be wasted. My motto became: *Nothing will be wasted. Everything will work together for good.*

My attitude set me on a path of restoration.

Chapter 5

Fleeing the Wall of Fire

I MOVED FORWARD, in spite of my grief.

Taking care of insurance details and planning the rebuild in the first month after the fire consumed my time. I met frequently with our builder, Scott, to work out the details of the new house. Our homeowner's association conducted endless meetings, which were important to attend. My responsibilities provided a structure I could depend on. When I used the logic-business part of my brain, my emotions quieted. Organizing and handling detailed tasks allowed me to temporarily avoid my emotions.

However, those feelings about my loss caught up with me any time I was alone, especially when I crawled into bed at night.

Still, I relished rare quiet moments by myself. I found comfort in spending time at the site of my burned house—a kind of gravesite—a tangible place to grieve.

About three weeks after my first visit, I sat in the shade of the skeleton of the largest pine in our backyard—now a charred trunk with crispy-brown needles on black branches—and stared at the remains of our home.

Journaling about my experience brought closure to each stage of my grief. Writing became one of my keys to healing as I put words to my deep sorrow and loss. That day, my writing took the form of a song. I called it the Restoration Prayer.

Journal Entry

July 2012
(one month after the fire)

Restoration Prayer

The trees tell the story of a fire roaring through.
Beautiful trees once standing now skeletons remain.

Ribbon of Your Presence, come to this place. Find your way through the ashes to touch this parched place. Touch each pile of rubble with your sweet embrace. Restore beauty from the ashes. Let this place be a song of grace.

We are broken-hearted, torn from so much grief, as we sift through the ashes and stand upon this loss. Staring at the rubble, nothing to say, searching for a treasure, does anything remain?

Ribbon of Your Presence, wind your way around our hearts, for our emptiness screams anguish as we reach to touch what's lost. May the memories that haunt us turn to treasures to hold dear.

We are broken-hearted, seared from so much grief. As we begin a chapter of building something new, excavate the darkness and heal our hearts anew.

Ribbon of Your Presence, restore this broken place. May the beauty from the ashes be the song to declare Your grace.

New Friendships Softened Our Grief

The same day I wrote "Restoration Prayer," I noticed one of my neighbors up the hill as she dug through the rubble of her house alone. I recognized her somber posture from one hundred yards away—as if her grief was a memorial cast in layers of despair. I made my way through the debris to join her.

We connected immediately, two women standing together in the remains of the homes that had once nurtured us. I told her about the song I had just written and sang it to her. The words brought tears to her eyes. Meeting this lady began the process of building a support system that would nurture me and others. I met many new friends who would become very dear to me.

Of the 32,000 people evacuated, most returned to their intact homes. Those who had no personal loss expressed their sympathies to those of us who did. Others returned to damaged or destroyed homes, some worse than others. Each of the 347 homes that burned represented a family—now homeless, many brokenhearted. I was only one of hundreds who had a total loss.

The fire affected everyone in different ways and gave each of us a unique story. Many people didn't want to talk about the tragedy; talking about a traumatic event opens vulnerable places where injuries hurt. Some who had lost everything held on tight to one of the few things they had left—their story.

As I built relationships after the fire, I heard many of those stories. Over time, I realized that people's experiences were even more precious than the irreplaceable heirlooms I had packed before the evacuation. So I set out to safeguard and preserve the stories about their changed lives.

I greatly cherish these personal accounts because the individuals opened their wounds to give strength to others, and I could tell it wasn't easy to give the gift of vulnerability. Susan was one of the first to share what had happened to her.

Susan's Story

Shortly after the great Waldo Canyon fire was extinguished, I met Susan at a women's support group, which we would later name the Wonderful Waldo Women. This band of heroines became an integral part of my support system and a great help for all the other ladies as well. A year later, when I decided to write a book, Susan agreed to meet with me and share her story. We met at a restaurant and she laid open her story of suffering.

A year and a half before the fire, Susan's thirty-four-year-old daughter, Kimberlie, died in her sleep from unknown causes. Eight weeks later, her son-in-law died at age forty-two from a massive heart attack.

Susan had already raised five kids of her own and still had a teenage daughter at home. With her strong character and loving heart, she brought her four orphaned grandsons, ages seven through fifteen, home to Colorado Springs to raise during what should have been her empty nest years. Having gone through a divorce a couple of years before the fire, she was raising them all as a single mom.

Just as the newly joined family had settled into their lives, the fire burned everything.

Susan's still-raw pain engulfed me, so I feared to hurt her with questions. In that moment, I decided the interview was over and I wanted nothing more than to comfort her. I didn't expect to add her story to this book because when she talked about her loss, memories dredged up almost insufferable pain for her. While I stopped asking her questions, she continued to share her story because she hoped others would benefit from her grief. For her story we are blessed.

Susan had lived in Mountain Shadows for eighteen years. That was where she had raised her children and would raise her grandchildren, too.

That fateful day, Susan saw flames through the dark smoky cloud on the ridge above her house. The fire had sounded like a train thundering toward her neighborhood. The encroaching danger had overloaded her senses. "I will never forget the smell of the fire, burned things."

Her family tried to get the dogs out of the yard and into the car. "The dogs freaked out," she told me. "My daughter and I crammed stuff into the car because we hadn't packed anything—we didn't think we would lose our house. I ran upstairs and grabbed the hard drive to the computer. I looked around my enormous home. *What should I get—my mother's china, my grandmother's silver?* I felt so overwhelmed, I took the refrigerator magnets and I left everything else."

At one point before escaping, Susan tried to take in the apocalyptic scene. She took photos, the urgency of leaving forgotten. But then her daughter yelled at her to get into the car. Just at the moment of departure, flames cropped up on the grass. Susan yelled at her neighbors to leave. "Go—the fire will get you!"

Susan and her daughter drove to a nearby middle school and watched the mountain burn. "It looked like bombs going off when each home was engulfed in flames." Each explosion made her ache as she realized another family's memories were on fire.

Kristin's Story

Kristin was also part of the support group where I met Susan. A busy mom of three and a teacher, we related as moms and teachers, holding our families together the best we could. I felt like I'd known Kristin for years.

The day the fire started, Kristin's family of five was on a camping trip and out of cell phone range. They didn't know that the Colorado Springs evacuation was underway.

"On our return home, we drove out of the canyon. Immediately, our cell phones started chiming. We listened to ominous messages, 'If you need a place to stay, let us know.' We called a neighbor to find out about the fire. After being briefed, we returned home and packed the four P's—people, pets, prescriptions, and important papers. My only job was to keep the kids calm. Their safety was all I really cared about."

Thomas' Story

I met Thomas at a Starbucks nine months after the fire. When I told him about the book I was writing, he was eager to help me out. He wanted to talk with me at his home, which was situated on a ridge overlooking the whole area, to explain his experience of events from his vantage point on the ridge.

We walked around his property as Thomas related his story. Reliving the tragic event together created a bond of friendship—the kind of friendship where we will do anything to support each other.

Thomas, a protector by nature, is a retired cop from the Los Angeles Police Department and a Marine veteran. He had always guarded his neighborhood with sincere vigilance.

"I packed some photos, papers, and a few guns, but stayed a little longer to surveil the neighborhood. An hour after the police came to evacuate, a truck with four or five dubious-looking men yelled for me to leave. I was concerned for my neighborhood and, not knowing the intentions of those men, I strapped on my 9mm gun and walked around my yard. In my world, protection is important. My neighbors trust me to watch over the neighborhood." Thomas left only after a police car came up his street and ordered him to go.

Hours later, he and his son, Brian, watched through binoculars (from a golf course overlooking the city) as his house burned.

"From the hill, I saw my house perfectly," he said. "I also had a clear view of most of my neighborhood and the homes up the block. My own home looked fine, but twenty minutes later, a cloud of smoke descended on the whole neighborhood. When the smoke cleared, two fires were burning right where I'd seen my house twenty minutes earlier.

I said to my son, 'My house burned to the ground.'"

His son agreed.

Thomas swallowed back his pain.

Thomas had lived through horrific scenes throughout his careers as a Marine and a cop, so his emotional response to the destruction of his home surprised him—the tough guy who always protected others.

Rudy's Story

I met Rudy, commonly known as Dr. Rudy, about two years after the fire. He taught a class on inner healing that I attended. He helped me work through still-unresolved emotions triggered by the fire.

The Waldo Canyon fire had a profound impact on Dr. Rudy, too. He gained an interesting perspective on the event and a compassionate heart for its victims. Dr. Rudy and his wife, Lynn, had recently relocated to Colorado Springs from California. They had settled into their rental house in preparation for beginning their counseling ministry. Their rental house was already furnished, so Rudy and Lynn kept their own furniture and most of their earthly possessions stacked in the garage.

Dr. Rudy had been conducting a counseling session in his home office when, through a window, he saw flames on the crest of the mountains above his home. He became instantly wary, but thirty minutes into the session, the flames had seemingly disappeared...but only because the flames had moved over the mountain.

Bullhorns sounded and police drove around to warn residents, "You have one hour to evacuate!"

The owner of Dr. Rudy's house, who lived in China at the time, called him. "Sometimes I get my mail late and I overlooked the insurance bill. There is no policy in place for the house. You have to get a crew together and cut down the trees around the house and try to save it."

"Wait a minute. I've got everything I have amassed during my life out in your garage," Dr. Rudy replied. "We agreed that you were going to cover my belongings on your insurance policy. I don't have renter's insurance."

The owner said, "We have no ability to put it into effect for at least a week."

Dr. Rudy began to panic, worried particularly about the two computers full of ministry information he and Lynn couldn't reach, as they were buried somewhere in the ceiling-high stacks of boxes. Also lost in the stacks were their family pictures and his collection of rare artifacts from WWI and WWII. "I called my pastor and asked if we could get a crew together to cut down the trees, but there was no time." As he and Lynn drove away, he thought, *My whole life's collection is threatened.*

Carolyn's Story

Carolyn organized the women's support group I attended after the fire. Our sons knew each other from school. Carolyn

welcomed me and the others to our meetings with a kind heart
and warm smile. Carolyn and I bonded as women with similar
pasts—both of us survivors and overcomers.

Carolyn and her family were celebrating her husband's sixtieth
birthday at their cabin in the mountains when a friend called
and alerted them to the fire in Waldo Canyon. They rushed home.

As soon as they arrived, Carolyn started packing, even
though they had not been ordered to evacuate. "My husband
must have thought I was crazy, but he didn't say anything. I
had a bad feeling and shook in fear while I instructed my family what to pack."

Their house had no air conditioning and the smoke was
too thick to open the windows, so Carolyn sweated while she
videotaped the contents of the house three times, wanting to
make sure she didn't miss anything in case her house did burn.
After packing, they left for a friend's home, which had air conditioning, a welcome refuge from the sweltering heat.

They unloaded three carloads of belongings into their
friend's basement and then watched the fire from the pool at
the Garden of the Gods Club. "We hardly talked. We stared at
the billowing mountainside and wondered if our house would
burn down."

Their youngest son, Jeff, remained with Carolyn and her
husband. Their two older boys returned to their respective
homes in Denver and California.

The next day, Carolyn, her husband, and Jeff returned home
because the fire had shifted away from their neighborhood,
making it safe to return. They spent the night at home and
even started unpacking. Carolyn made a list of what she put
away in case she needed to grab it again.

Around 2:00 p.m. the next afternoon, they loaded more stuff

into their cars. According to news reports, the fire had shifted toward them again. Even though their street hadn't been given the evacuation order yet, people living just two streets over were under mandate to leave. But at Carolyn's place, the phone hadn't rung with a reverse 911 call nor did the fire department knock on their door to warn them.

The fire returned. And it surprised everyone.

"I was in my closet, picking clothes," Carolyn told me. "This top or this top?" Then she heard her son scream, "MOM! DAD!" and she ran downstairs.

Jeff cried out, "Look at this! It's all the way down the hill. We've got to go!"

They jumped into their car with what they had already packed and left everything else, fleeing the wall of fire, hardly able to see or breathe due to the smoke.

Deb's Story

I have known Deb since 2005, when she was the principal of the school where I taught. We worked together until she retired two years later and our friendship has grown ever since. On the day when authorities gave the pre-evacuation warning, Deb called and invited us to stay with her. We declined because we didn't need a place to stay.

Ironically, almost a year later, on June 11, 2013, the Black Forest fire of Colorado threatened Deb's farmhouse, stunned our community, and eclipsed the Waldo Canyon fire as the worst in Colorado history. Close to five hundred homes burned and two more residents lost their lives.

I remember the day the Black Forest fire started. Early that morning, I was sitting outside on my patio having a cup of coffee. Hot air blew on my face and an eerie feeling pricked my senses.

This feels like a fire day. I wonder if firefighters and first responders think this is a normal day—it's not.

Later that afternoon, I saw smoke and parked my car in a grocery store lot overlooking the city. Other curious onlookers filled the parking spaces and stood on the ridge with me. We stared in disbelief and talked about our fears. The fire appeared to be in the direction of Deb's house. I checked the news and called Deb, who was already packing.

Deb and her husband, Denny, lived about twenty minutes northeast of my Manitou Springs home. Her daughter, son-in-law, and five grandchildren lived with them in their country home. Their farmhouse sat on several acres filled with llamas, goats, chickens, and dogs. Deb bred dogs because of her love for two uncommon breeds, Newfoundlands and Cavalier King Charles Spaniels.

Deb asked Denny if she should take the handmade bedspread she had made for him. The Civil War quilt had taken months to sew due to the many small pieces and detailed design.

"Everything you take," he said, "you're just going to have to put back. Everything will probably be okay."

Thirty minutes later, two police officers drove up to their house and instructed them to leave immediately. Deb told the police they would, just as soon as they loaded their dogs. The policemen drove away and Deb's three oldest granddaughters helped her load the little dogs into the small kennels they'd stacked in the horse trailer earlier. Deb handed the girls one dog at a time and they hurried back and forth to the horse trailer until all the little dogs were secured.

But the large dogs panicked. Denny and son-in-law, Mike, had to wrestle the one-hundred-and-sixty-pounders into the horse trailer with the Cavaliers. After all the dogs were secure, their four cars were lined up in the driveway, ready to leave. Deb's daughter, Holly, was in one car with the five children,

Mike was in another car, Deb was in another, and finally, there was Denny's car.

Deb spotted an orange glow across the street. It jumped. Flames were uncomfortably near.

"By then, fierce winds made my hair go sideways," she told me later. "I didn't realize it at the time, but we were in a firestorm. And firestorms have a distinct sound—a hum like a swarm of bees, but more intense."

Denny, though, didn't come out of the house as expected. He moved almost in slow motion—piddling around, closing and locking the windows—apparently thinking that now, no one could rob their house and the closed windows would contain a blaze if one part of the house caught on fire. Clearly, the stressful situation had traumatized Denny and dazed his senses. He had lost perspective and wasn't fully grasping the imminent danger.

The police knocked on the door a second time and told Deb they *had* to go now.

"I didn't know what to do because I had already gone in several times to get Denny. I told my daughter to leave."

Holly said, "No! We are *not* leaving Dad!"

Deb told the policemen, "If you want him out, you are going to have to get him out, because he's not coming."

Two policemen drove up close to the house and ran through the garage and into the house. They came out with Denny. He got in his car, which was hooked up to pull the horse trailer.

All four cars followed Deb. "I couldn't see the road because of the smoke," she told me. "I followed the lights on the police cars. The wind shifted and the fire headed toward us." As they turned left out of their driveway, Deb didn't know the fire was split into two fingers. They drove away in the middle of the two fingers.

The cars went north to the next street. They all turned right, away from the fire, except for Denny's car. The smoke disoriented him and he turned left. "We got a half a mile up the road and waited for Denny. He didn't come. I said, 'Where's Dad?' We waited and he didn't follow."

Deb signaled the others to go ahead and she went the opposite direction to find Denny. "Blockades guarded the road. I went around the barriers. Officials told me I shouldn't go, but I went anyway. After a frantic search, I spotted the horse trailer and found Denny coming out of a Popeyes Chicken with a tub full of chicken under his arm as if nothing was happening."

"What are you doing?" I asked.

"I thought we would need supper."

Our Reactions Surprised Us

We can't predict how we might react to a traumatic situation. Some people were able to think with clarity at the time of the evacuation. But the gravity of events hit them later. Others responded out of their normal character. They wouldn't have recognized themselves if they saw a video of their responses to the evacuation.

No matter how we reacted, fleeing the wall of fire changed us.

Chapter 6

First Responders in Action

WHEN I INTERVIEWED Dr. Rudy about his experience of the evacuation, he offered helpful perspective.

"No matter how prepared people think they are, they are never really prepared for a devastating event," Dr. Rudy said. "Disaster doesn't happen in slow motion. There is no time to gather what you need—or want. Some people are lulled by having insurance and the thought, *It will never happen to me, anyway....*

"Pearl Harbor was a sudden disaster. Men were asleep on the boats. Others saw Japanese planes flying over, but didn't expect the attack because the United States wasn't at war. Bombs dropped. Ships sank and so did our men. It happened so fast no one had a chance to react."

The voracious appetite and constantly-changing direction of the Waldo Canyon fire overwhelmed our whole community. Even though we had emergency systems in place for massive destructive events, the fire still overpowered our resources. Our firefighters, many of whom were volunteers, had never fought a fire of this magnitude or duration.

The Evacuation of Manitou Springs
Reverend Hunting's Story

Reverend David Hunting, Public Information Officer for the Manitou Springs Fire Department and former pastor of the First Congregational Church in Manitou Springs, met with me at the fire station three years after the fire. During the Waldo Canyon fire, Rev. Hunting had managed the Fire Department's communications and thus, had witnessed the events as they unfolded. When he spoke, the present faded and transported us back to those awful days we both recalled with intense emotions.

The tragedy began for Rev. Hunting while he was preparing his Sunday sermon in the church sanctuary. He walked outside and saw the large cloud of smoke over Waldo Canyon.

"That doesn't look good," Hunting said aloud to himself.

"That night, there must have been about thirty firefighters on call, many of whom were volunteers. We planned for the worst, including evacuation procedures. We decided that the trigger event for evacuation would be if Williams Canyon, the throat leading into Manitou Springs, caught fire."

The team monitored the fire closely that night. About 11:00 p.m., Rev. Hunting went home, which was at the base of Red Mountain on the south end of town. At 11:30 p.m., he saw the fire racing down Williams Canyon. His daughter got close enough to take photographs.

"Around midnight, I took her photos down to the station and showed them to the fire chief," said Hunting. "At 12:30 a.m., we ordered the evacuation of Manitou Springs."

The decision to evacuate 5,000 people was a courageous call. To reach everyone in the shortest amount of time, they divided the town into sections and split into teams. Starting with the section closest to Williams Canyon, volunteers on foot and in cars knocked on every front door to deliver the evacuation order.

In response, a steady stream of cars fled the town via Manitou Avenue between 1:00 and 3:00 a.m. Everyone left in an orderly way. By daybreak on Sunday morning, the town was deserted. The cooperation and understanding attitude of our community amazed Rev. Hunting.

"I helped in the far west part of town," added Hunting. "Up in the mountains, a family who had a lot of horses needed help to evacuate. At about 3:00 a.m., I went up to help them load their horses. Live embers were falling from the sky, a sign the fire was very close. That threat put the fear of God in me—one ember could ignite the dry grass and our town would go up in flames. Thank God it didn't!"

After a night of directing the evacuation and battling the blaze, the firefighters were dead tired and desperately needed some sleep. Rev. Hunting invited them, "The church is open. You may sleep in the pews if you would like to."

Rev. Hunting had never missed a Sunday in the twenty-four years he had pastored the Congregational Church of Manitou Springs. "I wasn't going to miss church that Sunday either, even though I knew no one would be there."

At service time, he walked into the sanctuary. "I found at least a dozen firefighters fast asleep on the pews, exhausted beyond belief. I choked up. Before me, brave men and women who had put their lives on the line lay asleep in God's church. I felt the presence of God."

Monitoring the Fire

Later that day, Rev. Hunting and two firefighters drove up Highway 24 toward the fire to assess the situation. Otherwise deserted, Highway 24 was staged with a fire engine every 500 feet.

"Our firefighters were watching for hot spots and falling embers where fire might ignite. On the side of the road, smoldering remnants of the fire still burned. The eerie sight took my breath away," said Hunting.

The next day, he and his team went to Cave of the Winds, which had a clear view of the fire areas. As they looked down toward Waldo Canyon, they saw flames break across 500 yards of grass and explode into flames.

"It's impressive and humbling how Mother Nature and fire can take control of a piece of real estate in an instant," he commented.

On Monday, Day Three of the fire, Rev. Hunting left for a briefing with the Manitou Springs Police Chief, the Assistant Fire Chief, and the El Paso County Sheriff. They drove up to the staging post at Holmes Middle School.

"While we were standing on the ridge, the mushroom cloud above the fire exploded into a frightful mass. In a few minutes, the fire ripped through Queens Canyon and into Mountain Shadows. A high-pressure front caused the smoke column to collapse in on itself, driving the wind down the canyon. Like blowing on campfire embers, the gusts of hot air fueled the inferno."

When they got back in the car, Rev. Hunting felt the tension amplifying. "Each of us knew this was going to be a bad night. We didn't know how bad the impending threat really was until we got back to the station."

Structures Burn in Mountain Shadows
June 26, 2012

Wind gusts of sixty-five miles per hour drove the fire east through the steep slope of Queens Canyon and into residential neighborhoods. Everything had happened so quickly neither the firefighters nor residents comprehended how far east the fire had already come.

When Rev. Hunting heard that the fire now threatened the neighborhood where both his mother and mother-in-law lived (on Centennial by Flying W Ranch), he told his wife to get their moms out of there. She succeeded, but barely escaped herself due to the backed-up traffic.

Mrs. Hunting called her husband as she drove. "The fire is on the grass area by Chipita School and there is fire right next to my car." Her call was sobering—the chaos he was managing at work now threatened his own family.

"Manitou Springs Fire Department was one of the first to be staged at that awful, awful fire," Rev. Hunting said. "When Mountain Shadows blew up, eight or ten of our crew were on that fire line. They had staged fire engines along Flying W Ranch Road with a few other units from Colorado Springs. I monitored the situation from the station. Over the radio, I heard the firefighters…"

"This is Engine One. The house I've been protecting is safe, but another one three doors down just blew up."

"Need more units. Fire spreading."

"This house is gone. That house we can save."

"Good job. You just saved that house."

"Water pressure from hydrants is dropping."

Rev. Hunting had even heard reports of firefighters seeing huge pillars of blue flames shooting up from backyard grills as propane tanks exploded ten to twenty feet in the air.

When his crew returned to the station about 4:00 a.m., he had never seen more exhausted people come out of a fire truck. "I put my hand on one of the trucks—it was still warm from being near the fire. As their chaplain, I gave all the dead-tired workers a big hug and said, 'God bless you.' These are tremendously brave individuals who put themselves in harm's way to save a lot of people and homes."

After our interview, I asked Rev. Hunting a couple of questions related to my personal story. We looked at a map and realized the Manitou Springs fire engines that had been staged on the Flying W Ranch Road fire line were likely the ones that had tried to save my yellow house. Tears welled up in my eyes. I felt humbled to know the brave firefighters who sacrificed to help me and others.

I also asked him about the UCCS meeting and why we had had to wait so long for news about our homes in Mountain Shadows. He told me that officials had literally scrambled over and around the rubble of every neighborhood to account for every address and to ensure every homeowner would have correct information.

Evacuation of the Mountain Shadows Area
Sergeant Benner's Story

Sgt. Benner and I spoke at the Colorado Springs Police Department two years after the fire. His professional attitude and willingness to freely share his perspective as a first responder shed light on what had happened behind the blockades.

I left feeling proud we have people of his integrity serving our city.

Police officers fight crime, not fires. While they weren't familiar with working in smoke, heat, and flame, they were the manpower we badly needed to evacuate residents and direct traffic.

Sgt. Benner evacuated neighborhoods and directed traffic for much of the day while the Waldo Canyon fire ravaged residential neighborhoods. He normally worked in the Gang Unit, which frequently worked with SWAT teams to support their critical missions. Commanders had informed his team they might be sent in to help evacuate neighborhoods, depending on how the winds changed or how bad the fire got. His team had a Plan A, Plan B, and a Plan C.

Plan D became necessary.

Sgt. Benner told his story. "My partner and I lit our lights and sirens to get up to Flying W Ranch, an area we weren't familiar with because we usually worked in another area of town. A grainy fog covered the area with super-smoky air that made my eyes water. Taking even small breaths burned my mouth and throat. We checked our maps to find the streets we were assigned to and, systematically, walked door-to-door warning residents to get out. The thick smoke made it difficult to see the house numbers we needed to radio in. Dispatch recorded which residents were contacted."

Suddenly, a fire truck appeared.

One of the firefighters said to Sgt. Benner, "Get out of here, now! Fire is about to explode right here!"

That's when he saw the golden-red wall of fire come over the mountain. Quickly, he got his team together by radio and they headed out. But he took a wrong turn and they ended up in a cul-de-sac. Luckily, no one had followed them.

Although they had seen no flames on the way into the cul-de-sac, seconds later when exiting, fire surrounded them on both sides of the street. "Embers fell on our cars—some the size of footballs. Fire blew up everywhere. How did the fire get there when just a few seconds before there had been none? In our daily work, we don't deal with fires—we were awestruck."

Traffic had stopped. Hundreds of cars were lined up trying to get out. Flames flared up on the grass next to the cars. A hail of fire embers ignited new blazes everywhere the wind willed them.

Benner now realized there was no traffic control. His team went to work, getting everyone as far away from the fire as possible. Once they got the first few cars going south on both sides of the road, others followed. Most of the people impressed him because they understood the severity of the situation and co-operated, even while panicked.

"If we told them, 'You need to go this way,' they did."

After the traffic was under control there, Sgt. Benner and his team left and evacuated another area. However, some people who had lost touch with their family members or wanted to rescue their pets were desperately trying to get back into their evacuated neighborhoods, ignoring police commands to stop.

Benner told me, "We couldn't let them in because if they got hurt, that would be on us. I understood that people were freaked out and desperate to locate their loved ones. But we had to make people understand they could not go back in."

Calm Out of Chaos

First responders were the calming force that brought order to the many desperate, frightened citizens. "As a whole, this city bucked up," Sgt. Benner said. "They pulled up their britches and made vital adjustments to make sure the general public was safe. Our plan was in place, but it got fractured. But our officers didn't panic. No one ran. No one left. After the fire forced them out of neighborhoods, officers took it upon themselves to find other areas that needed to be addressed. They provided the necessary leadership to get the job done. It was a miracle more people did not die or get hurt."

As we continued our interview, Sgt. Benner's words resonated with me. *If people got hurt, that would be on us.* He had assumed responsibility for every citizen. He and his team, along with all the first responders, hadn't hesitated to place themselves near the flames of the firestorm.

Our public servants had proven their core values extended far beyond the call of duty.

First Responders Directed—Citizens Fled

When people evacuated, they weren't prepared mentally or physically for the emergency. Some residents didn't have a chance to pack. They fled the wall of fire with frightened pets in their arms while their neighborhood blazed in the rearview mirror.

For many families, the dark clouds of smoke had blurred their vision and swallowed up their past. Loaded vehicle after vehicle had fled, full of anxious faces, some with children clinging to their parents. Other folks had to escape alone, exiting with the little they had been able to gather. Some had packed as if they were only leaving for a sleepover and afterward, lived with the regret of not taking more of their possessions.

They had escaped the firestorm, but now were facing an uncertain future. And with it came the hardest part— the waiting.

Chapter 7

Not Knowing Is Worse
Than Bad News

NOT KNOWING CAUSED the worst kind of anxiety.

We wondered, *Did my home burn down completely? If not, what is left of it and my possessions?*

Then we asked ourselves, *Where will I stay? How long will I be displaced?*

Many family members had been separated and reuniting was difficult due to overloaded communication systems and changing evacuation orders. Evacuees had fled to hotels, friends' basements and guest rooms, or temporary shelters in high school gyms and churches. Some residents had retreated to one area, only to be forced to leave again as the fire shifted. Sometimes, plans for safe haven evaporated altogether.

Making things even worse for some, searches for beloved pets, which had hidden in fear, made a quick exit difficult. Some families had simply been forced to leave without their pets.

Uncertainty dominated as strongly as the firestorm itself. Each forced relocation underscored the lack of safety and control; it was as if we were being chased by the willful, deadly fire.

Waiting felt like being pulled under by an ocean wave, helpless against the force of the current. No matter how hard I fought the wave, it consumed me until—it finally let me go.

Knowing was the release.

Knowing my home had burned down was better than not knowing. For the answers—even if they were unpleasant—

gave me resolve. Knowing told me which way to go, and having a direction gave me a sense of control.

Susan: Truth Versus Denial

Because Susan had seen the flames as she left her neighborhood, she suspected her house had burned. Still, she hoped for the best. No one actually knew for certain which houses had been destroyed.

At that time, Susan's son, Logan, was serving as a Marine in Afghanistan. He had access to satellite photos the media didn't have. He called his mom on her cell, "It looks like a giant stomped on our house."

After the call from Logan, Susan went to the same meeting at UCCS I attended. She flipped through the same list of addresses in her stapled packet, but her address wasn't on it.

Her heart leapt with hope for a few seconds...maybe? But deep inside, Susan knew the truth. She just couldn't fathom that her home was really gone. (In spite of the officials' careful work, her corner house was inadvertently missed.)

When she finally spoke to her neighbor, who had served as an on-site police officer during the fire, she learned that he had, indeed, witnessed her house burn.

Kristin: We Sensed That Our House Had Burned

Photos and footage of the fire had dominated the media. To protect their children from unnecessary stress, Kristin and her husband wouldn't turn on the television until their kids were in bed. That way, they wouldn't be frightened by the disturbing images of the fire and the destruction around them.

"That was probably the smartest decision we made," they said. "We had a strong sense our house had burned. As a family, we discussed whether we would rather have our house up or down. All five of us agreed—we would rather have it down.

We couldn't live with the guilty feelings of having a house that survived among all the others that burned."

Kristin's family learned on Wednesday morning, three days after the fire started, that their house was truly gone. "We scrolled through the *Denver Post* photos online and found a photo of our house in flames."

Kristin's intense sadness at the loss emerged later, at the notification meeting at UCCS. When Kristin saw the numbers of her address in print, *DESTROYED*, the tragedy produced another, stronger level of emotion. Her emotions broke through the shock. Devastation moved from her head to her heart. It was real.

Thomas: Turn of Events

Thomas had watched his home become enveloped in smoke and assumed the worst. The next day, an aerial photograph showed, in fact, that his home had not burned. Elated his house had survived, Thomas also felt miserable because his neighbors' homes hadn't.

Thomas grasped their pain. Afterward, his neighbors' devastation so near to his own unharmed house reminded him daily of their suffering.

Dr. Rudy: Kindness and Sanctuary

Rudy's face lit up as he told me one of his stories. After he and Lynn evacuated their home, they stopped at the Chick-fil-A drive-thru for a drink. The order taker asked if they were evacuees. When Rudy said yes, the order taker said they could have anything on the menu for free. Rudy and Lynn were surprised and heartened by this act of kindness.

"A family from church put us up in their house while they were on vacation," he said. "We watched the television news constantly to follow the direction of the fire. It never did come into our area, but the cops wouldn't let us go back to our home.

I tried again when they started allowing other people to return, but our road was still blocked. Because we had heard about several thefts in our neighborhood, our anxiety was, of course, pretty high. And since it took five or six days before we were allowed back in our home, when we finally did arrive, we were elated."

Carolyn: Did Our Home Survive?

"We went up on top of a hill and watched the smoke roll in. It was so thick, we couldn't see a thing. *Is that our house burning? Or someone else's house?*

"We didn't know for days whether our house had burned down or not. We looked at a Google map, but couldn't tell. We went to the mandatory meeting at UCCS to get info, but our address was not on the list. That gave us a little bit of hope.

"But we left the meeting not knowing for certain. The fact that everyone else knew if their house made it and we didn't bothered me. How could officials have made a mistake like this?

"The next day, I went to the roadblock where the National Guard was monitoring the burned area. I found a policeman and said, 'Excuse me, we aren't on the list from UCCS, but from Google Maps, it looks like our house could be gone. Would you mind going in and looking to see if it's there?' I gave him the address and he drove up the hill.

"When the officer returned, he said, 'I'm sorry, ma'am—your house is gone.'

"*It was final.*"

Deb: I Didn't Think Our Home Could Have Survived

"I thought our house probably had burned because the last time I looked back, I saw the fire ablaze on the road next to my house. I didn't think our home could have survived.

"The next day, fire officials shared a list of addresses of destroyed homes. One of my six children called me when they saw our address on a website or a gap in a photo where our house should have been. I must have been numb because I don't remember which child called me or what they said.

"Some addresses were mistakenly left off the list—so many families had false hope their homes had survived. Later, they discovered the bad news. I felt sorry for those people."

Ann: Gracious Support From a Survivor

Ann's home had burned down twelve years earlier in Los Alamos, New Mexico. Knowing what difficulties we faced, Ann graciously offered support to those of us who were suffering the effects of the Waldo Canyon fire.

Using Skype, she joined our women's support group meeting via video conferencing. She gave us hope, saying she had recovered and we would, too. We clung to her every word. Ann spoke from experience and clearly knew how we felt.

Ann echoed our feelings that *not knowing* was one of the worst parts of her fire story. When I interviewed her, she recalled the in-between time—when they waited for news on her house. She and her husband, Steve, stared at the television, desperate to know whether their house had survived.

"*Not knowing* was the greatest torture," Ann said. "The only news we received was from the helicopter fly-overs that showed an aerial view." As they strained to see their house among the others, they became exasperated because the helicopter habitually turned the corner before it got to their house.

Finally, Ann's husband called the news station and asked them to fly farther so they could see.

At last, the aerial view showed their house.

Burned to the ground.

"I felt relieved to finally *know*," Ann said. "Our home was gone. Knowing was much better than remaining on the brink of an emotional cliff. Once we realized our house was destroyed but we were still alive, we could decide where to go next."

Ann's Evacuation

The fire that destroyed Ann's home in Los Alamos in 2000 had many similarities to the Waldo Canyon fire.

Erratic winds shifted constantly and evacuation plans changed with every shift in the fire's direction. One minute, residents thought they were safe; the next minute, they were in danger.

The Los Alamos evacuation had also flowed with remarkable calmness and order. An entire town had driven away from their homes with great anxiety, but only two reports of minor fender benders were noted.

Ann and Steve were somewhat fortunate, as they had had some time to pack.

The Cerro Grande fire had been started as a controlled burn several miles from Los Alamos by the National Park Service. When it got out of control, the part of Los Alamos nearest the fire was put under an evacuation order. Ann lived further away, but asked her husband whether he would think her silly to pack a few things.

"No, not at all," he said, so Ann gathered some things together and filled her husband's car.

A day or so later, the fire had begun to approach their neighborhood, then it suddenly shifted away. In response, officials cancelled the evacuation order.

"We heard that more evacuations were planned," Ann said to me. "I thought we could go out to our property on the far side of town and camp, so I gathered our camping supplies and loaded them in my car. But a policeman came to our door and told us that the entire town was evacuating and we must leave *now*.

"We grabbed our cat and left. We passed a park in the heart of town and the wind was blowing so hard that large branches snapped off the trees. I thought, *No wonder they are getting us out of here! The wind is blowing the fire toward us.*"

Sgt. and Beth Benner: Not Knowing Affected First Responders and Their Families Too

Residents who had escaped the fire were not the only ones living with the anxiety of *not knowing*. The spouses and families of our first responders had had little contact with their loved ones. The firefighters had been almost completely cut off, battling the fire monster somewhere deep in the thick smoke, trying to contain the beast.

Everyone clung to their cell phones and waited for news.

It didn't come often enough.

Sgt. Benner's wife, Beth, worked at a doctor's office on the side of town opposite from the fire. Her office kept the radio on and waited for updates. About two or three in the afternoon, her husband called, "Our worst fears have been confirmed—the fire has crested over the peak and it's coming down the other side. They're sending us in."

"What do you mean, they're sending you in? Where?"

"We have to knock on doors and get the people out."

When she was on her way home from work she saw the black-orange smoking rolling in fury. "Oh my gosh! He's in *that*!"

Later that evening, her sister called to comfort Beth, "Let's be real. He's a *police* officer. They won't send him into the fire."

Beth felt encouraged and stayed glued to the TV for updates. She waited for her husband to call so she could breathe a sigh of relief. Hour after hour passed...no call. Beth had finally fallen asleep when, sometime after midnight, he walked into their bedroom. He reeked of smoke, even though he had left his uniform in the garage.

"They sent you into the fire, didn't they?" she asked, needing no answer.

The next morning, Sgt. Benner remained asleep while Beth got up to take a shower. Black grime from the smoke covered the bathroom floor. She opened the shower door and gasped,

"What the heck?" Black streaks from his hands covered the entire shower stall.

Sgt. Benner went back to work later that day. At one point, he called Beth to fill her in on the details they hadn't had time to discuss earlier. When he told her they had sent him into the highest point of the fire, she suddenly realized the danger her husband had faced and nearly passed out.

Rev. Hunting: Community Spirit

Hundreds of firefighters from around the country came to fight the fire. Officials set up a command center at Holmes Middle School. A sea of pup tents splattered the landscape—each structure a beacon of both relief and alarm.

"In the early mornings, we met with the Incident Commander, Rich Harvey," Rev. Hunting told me. "He briefed us on that day's strategy for fighting the fire and then we were dismissed to our respective stations and posts about 8:00 a.m.

"One of our most heart-felt experiences was coming back home to the station along 31st Street by the Starbucks on Colorado Avenue. Dozens and dozens of people were holding up homemade signs expressing their thanks.

"Little kids stood on the streets by their mom's sides holding signs. 'We love you, daddy!' 'You're our heroes.' 'Thank You, Firefighters!' Citizens lined the streets and cheered for us as we drove by. Up and down Manitou Boulevard, businesses and residents posted signs thanking us for our service. Their gratitude meant a lot to the firefighters."

Our community stood together to support our brave ones who had been willing to fight for the safety of others and for their homes.

The loved ones of the first responders had also sacrificed.

Spouses, children, moms, dads, grandparents, and friends showed tremendous support for those who fought the dangerous fire. Each day, families and friends had been forced to wait for the safe return of their loved ones.

It was the waiting that was hard on all of us. But at last, the firestorm hushed and the ground cooled.

Then came the next phase—what to do with what remained.

Section Two

Excavation Comes
Before Restoration

Chapter 8

Returning Home Takes Courage

PEOPLE LIKE TO CONTAIN THEIR LIVES in neatly wrapped packages. But in an instant, life can change, disrupted forever. Unwelcome surprises can unravel our lives and crush our dreams.

I knew this well from past experience. The fire also taught me important truths. One epiphany I had was from a pile of rubble.

Rocks don't burn, right?

Well, mine did.

At least I have my rocks, I told myself. *They can be part of my new landscape after the debris is removed.*

My rocks meant a lot to me because they had survived the fire. I even smiled when I thought about rearranging them in my new yard after we rebuilt.

Just a few weeks after the fire, I met a landscaper at the burn site. I propped my foot up on a boulder as we discussed plans.

But I noticed a crack and looked closer.

I tapped the crack with my foot—a chunk of the boulder broke off. Looking closer, I saw a larger crack. I kicked the boulder and it split in half. Shocked, I stomped it over and over until it crumbled to little pieces.

Immediately, I went about testing each rock in the yard to see if they would crumble, too. They all did. Rocks are symbols of endurance, they're supposed to stand the test of time.

Realizing the frailty of things I had relied upon and my own inadequacy crumbled me.

But then I remembered what my Sunday school teacher taught me in my youth. I had memorized the scripture, *"The Lord is my rock, and my fortress."* (Psalms 18:2 King James Version) I still believed that to be true.

Seeing those rocks shatter under my feet showed me something new—earthly rocks may crumble, but my rock of faith endures.

My Lord is a rock that will never burn.

Journaling to Heal

My process of dumping emotion became a journey of healing. I bought a journal and called it my *fire book*. Writing brought closure—deliverance from unresolved pain.

My *fire book* had random quotes printed at the top of every fifth page. I remember the night I wrote the story about my crumbled rocks. The last two sentences I wrote before I turned the page to continue writing the rest of the story were the following: *At least I have my boulders, even though they are charred. Their presence gives me a sense of security.*

At the top of the next page was the following quote: *Faith is the cornerstone on which all great lives are built.*

Of all the profound quotes in the book, this one spoke to me like a whisper in my ear—a reminder that faith remains even when everything else burns.

Facing our flattened homes and the reality of what we had lost tore us apart. Each of us handled our grief in different ways.

Kristin: Memories and Hope

The day Kristin and Doug, her husband, were allowed to view the remains of their home, they first checked in at Eagle View Middle School to show proof of their address.

"We received a cooler filled with gloves and trash bags. My husband and I followed the line of cars headed to our neighborhood with knots in our stomachs, somberly anticipating what we would see. We turned the corner, one more street closer to home.

"Then we turned onto our street–Ashton Park Place. Our house was, literally, a ton of ashes. With great awe, we stood on our property and cried. The chaplain and firefighters met us on our lawn. The firefighters said they had been forced to leave our house twice because of the extreme heat. Our hearts sank. Our house had been so close to surviving...yet so far.

"The beam supporting our garage still stood, as did the north wall of our house and our wooden deck. And we found our dishwasher dangling, intact dishes still inside. But nothing else was salvageable.

"Hundreds of our books, now burned pages of confetti, littered the front and back yards. I made it my own little game to read fragments of lines from scraps of pages and guess the book title. It brought me great satisfaction to think about the memories attached to my children's favorite books. The memories were still mine—even though my fingers only touched their singed remnants.

"We found our fleece jackets melted together, our planter pots shattered with dirt spilling out, and our mailbox begging for a delivery."

As a way to process her pain, Kristin wrote down her thoughts. Her response to the loss of her home and belongings refreshed me. One of her quotes referred to a "hole of hope." That's because most Colorado homes have basements. When homes burned, the remains dropped into the hole of their foundations.

Kristin had stared into the hole of their house's foundation, filled with ashes and layers of her past.

"A million memories were tucked in my heart, not in my house. Still, I peered into the earthen shell, imagining the possibilities. It was our hole of hope."

Thomas: Painful Points of View

"Once I moved back into my home, the new view from my deck upset me. On my left, I saw ashes, ruins, and what looked like a war zone. The fire had destroyed everything. Even the homes on the horizon were flattened.

"On my right, I could see downtown Colorado Springs, where everything looked normal. The city was operating as if nothing had happened. So when I sat out on my deck, I tried to concentrate on the right side, where everything looked normal.

"But my eyes always gravitated left toward the area of destruction because I felt my neighbors' loss. I experienced tremendous sadness living on the ridge above, knowing I had friends below me and on my street with no homes."

Carolyn: Nothing Left But the Future

"Jim and I drove up the hill to the remains of our four thousand-square-foot house. Our house was GONE. Looking at the empty place where our house should have been was truly unbelievable. There was nothing left except the steps leading to the front entrance of the house and a window, which looked weird standing among the embers—like a portal into the future."

Deb: Nothing Else Mattered

Police cars had taken groups of people into Deb's ravaged neighborhood.

"A friend went with me because Denny was at work," she told me. "Fifty cars or more were lined up in a row behind the blocked-off streets. I was the only one there from my street, so a policeman escorted me and my friend alone. We waited two and a half hours to enter. When we did go in, the area looked like a war zone.

"We drove into my driveway and got out of the car. The ground was still warm from the fire; I could feel the heat through my shoes. The burned ground crunched when I walked.

"The only thing left of my house was the ceramic bulldog on the front porch. The bulldog—with its feet burned off—became important to me because nothing else had survived. I asked the policeman to put it in my car.

"I stared in disbelief that a large house full of solid things could be reduced to such a tiny pile. The destruction astounded me. My family and animals got out safely. Nothing else mattered. Nothing else ever has mattered or ever will. I didn't think about what I lost until later."

Ann & Steve: Angel in the Ashes

"We didn't know what we needed. The insurance company helped by thinking ahead for us. They provided supplies for us to return to our burned home: garbage bags, gloves, masks for the dust, and cell phones with paid minutes.

"Steve and I parked across the street and got out of the car. We walked to the end of the driveway and simultaneously both of us broke down. We hugged each other and cried. Then after a couple of minutes of tears, we said, 'Okay let's see what lies ahead.' At that point, we switched into adventure mode. We got the cry out of the way and proceeded to find out if we could salvage anything.

"We had left a car behind, now just a puddle of aluminum with a nest of wires from the steel-belted tires. Officials estimated that the fire was about two thousand degrees when it went through our house.

"The storehouse behind our house had not burned as hot. That's where I stored our Christmas ornaments, including some antique glass decorations that had been my grandmother's. In the ashes of the storehouse, I found one of the most special of those ornaments—my grandmother's angel. I held the angel in my hand. It lasted long enough for me to admire it, then it disintegrated into dust.

"I am so glad I had that moment. It gave me closure on some of the treasured items I lost."

Ann and Steve's positive spirits inspired me. They approached this tragedy as an unfolding storybook. Together they mourned and together they bravely took the next steps in their lives. They had each other and hope for whatever might lie ahead. They would make the best of it.

Facing the total ruin of our homes required courage. After we absorbed the shock of the physical destruction, we had to deal with the emotional impact from the trauma.

Some people struggled more than others.

Chapter 9

Thank God I'm Not Crazy— How Trauma Affects Us

Trauma turns lives upside down and inside out. One of the first steps to healing is understanding that our responses are normal reactions to abnormal events.

I saw whole blocks of beautiful homes flattened. Memories of the heartbroken faces of my neighbors stayed with me. Witnessing that level of mass destruction shook me deeply, conflicting with the rational part of my brain that enjoys routine and order.

Chaos delivered its message, "You have no real control." One second, everything was fine. The next second, everything changed. The fire reminded me that life is fragile, and so am I.

My losses affected me profoundly, but I put on a stoic face. A caretaker by nature, I gave others the impression I didn't need their support during those first weeks after the fire.

Helping others kept me busy. Taking action gave me a sense of purpose and strength when so many other people needed support. But busyness only deferred my pain temporarily— my emotions slowly unraveled in spite of my effort to contain them.

When I finally realized I needed support, I didn't know how to ask for it. I tried, but failed. Even my closest friends didn't comprehend what I was going through.

I had survivor's guilt.

Even though I had lost the yellow house that meant so much to me, I hadn't lost all my personal belongings like hundreds of others had. Because of this, I didn't feel worthy of compassion.

People's comments and responses to me were unfailingly predictable. It became obvious people felt helpless when standing next to someone who had lost everything. But learning that I still had my precious possessions instantly relieved them of the burden of compassion.

"My house burned in the Waldo Fire."

"Oh, I'm so sorry. How awful," they would gasp, a look of horror on their faces.

Feeling guilty, I would add, "We weren't living in the house at the time."

Relief flooded their faces as compassion for me evaporated— I wasn't one of the miserable people who had lost everything, after all.

Survivor's guilt told me I didn't deserve the compassion they offered and my shame told me I didn't want it. Little did I know how badly I needed it.

After a time, I learned to change the dynamic by saying, "My house burned, but I wasn't living in it at the time." I would say it fast enough so they didn't have time to give too much compassion.

Even years later, conversations with friends, acquaintances and strangers are exactly the same.

Nobody realized the gravity of my loss or my trauma— including me.

Why did I feel so devastated? I *felt* like I had lost everything, like the others. Why was I so torn up over losing a house when it was just a material thing that could be rebuilt?

Finding a Support System

The answers to these questions came later when post-traumatic stress disorder (PTSD) symptoms drove me to find a support system, a place to process my grief. There, I found the answers and keys to healing.

My neighbor told me about the women's support group where I would meet Susan, Carolyn, Kristin, and Ann a week later. My neighbor didn't make it that night, but the other women welcomed me and I immediately felt at home. We understood each other and bonded as common allies in our struggle to heal.

The second time I attended, we huddled in our support group, eager to be with familiar faces and to share our common grief. The heavy atmosphere lightened when Susan told her story about how she *lost* it. (Susan is always composed and proper, which made it all the more hilarious.)

Her story made me laugh for the first time since the fire, the kind of laughter that made me double over—and tear up.

Susan's Composure Cracked

Days after her house went up in flames, Susan was having one of those black days—you know, the kind where you are lucky to be standing because the weight of despair is so heavy.

Frustrated, Susan strode away from the home improvement store. None of the store's floor workers had been able to help her find the right shovel. The moment she stepped into the crosswalk, a man driving a sedan and in a hurry honked at Susan to scoot her across.

Are you serious? thought Susan. She swung her Brighton purse and shattered his headlight.

The man stared.

"Shame on you!" she scolded, and continued across the parking lot to her car. He froze, knowing by the look on her face not to mess with her.

It was so funny because we had all had "lost it" at one time or another, our raw emotions finally boiling over after simmering every day since the fire.

Deb: In the Fog

"After the fire, I felt like a bobble head....

"I would make plans and head to the other side of town. But often, I would have to pull over to the side of the road and ask myself, *Where am I going?* After sitting for a long while, I would remember. Arriving at my destination, I would forget again. More than once, I stood in the doorway of a store and knew I had a reason to be there, but couldn't remember why.

"I also struggled to hold a conversation. In mid-sentence, I would forget my train of thought. My disorientation felt creepy, like I was in outer space or something."

Ann: Losing It Over a Can of Beans

After staying with friends for ten days after losing their home, Ann and her husband were settling into their rental home. The house came fully furnished, with towels, bedding, and dishes, as they were renting from an artist who was living in Europe for a couple of years.

"We stopped at the grocery store on our way to our first evening away from our friends' home," she told me. "We decided on a simple meal of hot dogs and canned baked beans. Stopping at the store took the last of our energy. Exhausted, we set our groceries on the counter, eager to eat. I held the can of beans in my hand and looked for a can opener. We searched every drawer. Nothing. The fully furnished house did not have a can opener.

"The realization kicked me when I was already down. My pain burst into inconsolable sobs.

"I knew that someday I would laugh about *losing it* over a can of beans. That day came much later."

Overload From Trauma Magnifies Distraction

Many people I spoke with after the fire felt scatter-brained and unable to think clearly. Staying focused was a huge challenge and many of us wondered why.

Trauma overwhelms the senses. After experiencing an event that causes fear, helplessness, or loss, the brain expends massive amounts of energy to sort and process. Distraction is the result. A common example of distraction is walking into a room and not remembering why you are there. For trauma survivors, this type of distraction is constant and can continue for months, even years.

For months after the fire, I couldn't think straight. Normal activities became difficult. Many times when I drove alone, I had to pull off to the side of the road or sit in a parking lot because I couldn't make a decision. *Should I buy groceries? Should I go home?*

"Mom, don't forget to drop us off at school," my kids would cry from the back seat. This scenario happened frequently right after the fire. Time after time, I'd point my car in the right direction and then drive by my destination. My kids' reminders, even a year after the fire, surprised me that I was still so screwed up.

I simply couldn't focus because of trauma overload.

Reaching Out for Help

About two months after the fire, I was driving when one of those spaced-out moments overpowered me. I pulled my car over. *My distress can't be normal. I can't go on spacing out and crying.*

I already thought I needed professional support because, instead of getting better, these episodes were becoming more frequent. Right there, on the side of the road, I called a counseling referral hotline. I asked the attendant to find me someone who specialized in trauma and was immediately connected with a trauma counselor. We set up an appointment for the next day.

Christie Lee, a licensed clinical counselor, had worked as a trained trauma specialist for emergencies. She was the expert I had hoped for and needed.

I will never forget that first appointment when my survivor's guilt lifted. I had finally found a safe place to pour out my grief. I remember explaining that my house had burned—but that I wasn't living in it at the time and didn't understand my distress.

That appointment initiated the process of understanding and healing from my trauma. I don't remember exactly what she said, but remember feeling relieved. Christie Lee guided me to understand the weight of my losses. Her witness to my pain helped me let it go.

How Trauma Affects the Brain

Christie Lee also helped me understand how trauma affects the brain and its functions. She showed me images of brains from research done by Dr. Daniel G. Amen, a physician and psychiatrist with the largest database of functional brain scans related to behavior. The brain scans awed me because I saw visible evidence of the difference between normal brains and those impacted by trauma. This physiological explanation made sense and vindicated those of us with traumatized brains.

I remember thinking, *Thank God, I'm not crazy!*

Christie Lee explained, "When under extreme stress, the brain is literally hijacked. Trauma causes the amygdala, the emotional part of the brain, to swell like a balloon. The brain is saying, in effect, 'I am not safe, my world is ending.'

"When traumatized, communication between the left and right hemispheres of the brain stops. This is why we can't think straight. Effective problem-solving is over for the time being.

"For example, we have been told to count to ten when we're angry. Those few extra seconds can help calm the stressed amygdala and may help us avoid regrettable comments and reactions."

Experts Recommend Breathing to Restore Brain Activity

Christie Lee led me through specific breathing exercises that encourage the process of restoring normal brain activity. At the time, I took in the information and practiced the techniques she taught me at home. But I hated them. I'm not a sit-still kind of person and I didn't want to waste my time lying on the floor, slowly inhaling and exhaling. In our next few counseling appointments, I reported how annoying the breathing exercises felt.

I ignored her advice on breathing because I hated it so much until several months later, after I had done further research. My studies confirmed and expanded upon what I had learned from Christie Lee and gave me additional incentive to do the breathing exercises.

Understanding Fight or Flight

I also discovered that "spacing out" and "losing it" are symptoms of a highjacked amygdala, a term coined by Daniel Goleman in his book, *Emotional Intelligence*. The amygdala, an almond-shaped part of the brain, determines a fight, flight, or freeze response in a situation perceived as dangerous.

Here's how it works: The amygdala sends distress messages and temporarily cuts off the rational brain before it has time to respond. When in danger, it hijacks the rational, problem-solving part of the brain to protect us from immediate threat. This explains why people may react irrationally and/or destructively when emotionally triggered.

Understanding these concepts helped me make sense of the problems affecting a large community of traumatized people.

About a year after the fire, I took a class from an international organization called Day2. The founder, Victoria Jeffs, confirmed my research on brain function in trauma survivors and offered techniques in addition to the breathing exercises I had learned.

The curriculum she authored, *corePurpose: A Journey of Purpose* (formerly known as CrossRoads), explains how the immediate use of a game or exercise that requires logic forces the brain to move away from the triggered amygdala to the prefrontal cortex, the reasoning part of the brain.

She recommended exercises such as counting backwards from 100 by sevens. "Add the numbers on license plates. Add the number of letters in your name. Then add the letters in your family members' names."[4] She explained that thinking logically uses a different part of your brain, which stops the emotional experience. Thus, it halts the *hijacked amygdala*.

Information, then, gave me keys to healing. By learning technical information about the way traumatic events affect the brain, I gained a sense of control over an out-of-control situation.

And, knowing others were having similar experiences relieved some of the pressure of feeling alone in my suffering and confusion.

Annie's Insights Into Fight or Flight

Mayor Steve Bach and city officials set up a resource center named Colorado Springs Together for those affected by the fire. This non-profit organization rented a building in a central location to serve as a meeting place.

They hired Annie to serve as liaison and administrator for our ravaged community. Annie lived in Mountain Shadows and had been trapped as the fire came down the mountain. That experience gave her an understanding heart and her positive attitude made her the perfect person for the job. She met with nearly two thousand distressed people who came through the doors of Colorado Springs Together.

Annie's experience gave her deep insights into how people process trauma. "The *fight or flight* response in the face of a disaster is a common psychological theory of human behavior," Annie said.

She observed three types of people. "First, there are the fighters, the first responders, the people ready to lead a group and take charge—all of them leaders in some way. These people approached the crisis like a challenge to overcome and jumped into problem-solving immediately. These were the people who immediately took control in our homeowners' association when owners had no homes. Problem-solving clearly energized them.

"The next group froze in fear, deer in the headlights, paralysis by analysis. These people stared in awe at what had happened to them and around them. They watched everyone else react before making a single move. For some, moving forward took years.

"The third group of people simply left the day of the disaster; they never returned, never looked back. This group didn't talk about the trauma at all. When approached, they would change the subject—it was too painful to discuss. I know people who, three years after the fire, can't talk about their loss because the memories are too difficult.

"The bottom line is: Each type of person needs the other two groups to survive a tragedy. After the crisis calmed down, the fighters experienced a delayed grief reaction because they had been busy taking care of others. And those who had been frozen in fear were able to support the fighters in their time of need. Those people who had taken the time to work through their grief became stronger, enabling them to help others when they were ready to process their emotions.

"Most importantly, each individual responds in their own way and in their own time, and *no one* can dictate or should criticize their process."

Annie's advice reminded me of my mom's words when I was young: "People grieve differently. Be careful not to judge." Her wisdom prompted compassion in me for those who didn't act as expected. I remember the people who were angry. Thunder erupted out of them with every move they made and every word they spoke. Those around them stayed quiet. I was one of the quiet ones. The rumble of their anger made me feel afraid, but I understood that under their anger was unfathomable pain.

Personality Affects How We Process Stress

Different personalities respond to a crisis in different ways. Most typically, people handle trauma the way they handle other conflicts.

Leaders or drivers focus on meeting deadlines. Goals drive them. Feelings and deep thinking are a waste of time for such individuals, because they get in the way of making decisions. Other people view material things as tools to meet objectives, not objects with emotional attachments.

If there is a conflict at the office, some people will attack the problem to solve it, stepping on the toes of others to get the job done. These may be the people who keep meetings on topic and on schedule. Others need time to analyze and mull over every facet before they are ready to discuss the conflict. Others talk too much, making it difficult to get the job done. They have great ideas, but can't seem to focus.

I am one of the personality types that feel and think deeply. I notice details. I'm the person who saved every concert stub because the memory was special. I kept flowers from all of my high school proms and carefully stored them along with the dresses I wore. I refused to wash the dresses because I might wash off the magic from those special evenings in my life. Loss from the fire impacted me with more emotions than some others.

Beth described her response to the evacuation this way. "I was worried and frightened. But my husband looked at me and said, 'We have all we need—each other. We are all safe.' He pulled out his credit card, 'Whatever we need, we can buy.'" His logic and practicality refocused Beth and their children. His attitude made them feel safe.

People like Beth's husband focus on relationships. They are the people who don't attach meaning to things. For them, belongings are to be consumed or used to make more time for relationships.

Family of Origin Also Affects How We Handle Conflict

No matter which personality type you have, the way your family responded to conflict during your childhood influenced your reactions then and now in adulthood. For example, if a person grew up in a strong family unit that fostered security, he or she may manage stress and change with ease. Similarly, those who successfully dealt with frequent crises in their family of origin may navigate a natural disaster with more ease, because they learned conflict management skills while growing up.

The reverse is also likely; those from an unhealthy, chaotic family environment may have more difficulty dealing with a crisis, because they may not have learned healthy ways to manage them.

Insights from Annie and other resources answered many of our questions.

But knowledge could not ease the swelling pain that was about to burst out of me.

Chapter 10

What You Need to Know About PTSD

New trauma triggers past trauma.

Many people were already dealing with trauma and grief in their lives prior to the fire. Then catastrophic loss sent them into a tailspin.

Those struggling with post-traumatic stress disorder (PTSD) already had weakened coping mechanisms, so the new trauma from the natural disaster complicated their recovery.

I didn't feel safe and I couldn't get over it.

One sleepless night, before I called Christie Lee for support, I looked for answers on my computer. I needed an explanation as to why I was so freaked out about my house burning down. Finding a website about PTSD, I studied the list of symptoms. "Yep, have this one, yep, this one too. Oh my gosh—I have most of these symptoms! Why hasn't anyone told me I have PTSD?" I wanted to scream. At the same time, I felt relieved. I wasn't crazy, just wounded.

How many others were suffering with the same symptoms?

I wanted them to have the answers I had found.

What is PTSD?

Post-traumatic stress disorder is a mental health condition triggered by experiencing or witnessing a terrifying event. Symptoms include flashbacks, nightmares, and severe anxiety, as well as uncontrollable thoughts about the event.[5]

PTSD is more of a brain injury than an illness, because it is the brain's natural way of coping with an abnormal event. PTSD is actually the body's way of keeping one from being literally scared to death. In no way does having PTSD mean the individual has any kind of character flaw or weakness.

Symptoms of Post-Traumatic Stress Disorder in Adults*

- Feeling/being frozen and numb, with a desire to retreat from all stimulus that reminds the individual of emotionally charged events
- Not feeling connected to others or feeling disconnected from others
- Hypersensitivity to certain sensory stimuli like sounds, smells, movement, or visual reminders
- Difficulty sleeping, nightmares
- Hyper-vigilance, constantly being on guard, having a keen sense of the surrounding environment, purposefully detecting possible threats by scanning a room and looking for exits
- Avoidance through substance abuse or other self-destructive behavior
- Intrusive thoughts about the event. Difficulty concentrating because pictures or thoughts of the traumatic event invade and dominate one's thinking
- Inability to recall key facts about the traumatic event; loss of memory (not due to substance abuse or head injury)
- Aggressive behavior, unprovoked anger
- Loss of interest in activities enjoyed before the trauma
- Exaggerated startle response
- Easily annoyed by stimuli such as sound, movement, or having to respond in a conversation
- Flashbacks: pictures of previous unpleasant memories interrupt daily life; flashbacks can also be unpleasant feelings that are difficult to explain[6]

---

*This list of PTSD symptoms in adults is not exhaustive. Children display PTSD differently than adults. For more information on symptoms see: Diagnostic and Statistical Manual of Mental Disorders, Fifth Edition (DSM-5).

Body Memories

The mind may block out a traumatic event, but the body may remember at a cellular level.

This is why certain types of touch may trigger unpleasant memories from the past. While trauma survivors may not remember the traumatic event itself, their body may react to a touch that reminds them of the trauma. The following stories are a window into two survivors' actual experiences.

PTSD Survivor 1

"I feel it if I'm triggered. I feel it internally. I feel it emotionally, and the emotions become physical in my body. My stomach knots up. I freeze. I can't speak. Everything goes blank but primal fear. I seem to go back to the events emotionally with a physical manifestation."[7]

PTSD Survivor 2

"Every time I process trauma, I experience body reactions that were locked in at the time of each particular trauma. Reactions include getting sick to my stomach, having trouble breathing, cramping, pain, and other symptoms connected with the traumas I endured.

"I am lucky, though, because when I finish processing the trauma, the body memory related to the trauma also processes and disappears within a few days to a couple of weeks. Not the most pleasant experience, but I know there is an end, so I tough it out."[8]

What Can Trigger PTSD Symptoms?

Unexpected triggers can cause emotional outbursts or withdrawal when a person least expects it. When triggered by stimuli associated with the event, the body reacts as if the event is happening in the present. The sound of a siren may cause a person to panic if previously traumatized in an automobile accident. Being in a room painted a certain color may cause anxiety in someone who was repetitively abused in a room of the same color.

For me, both the smell of smoke and weather like we had during the fire trigger anxiety.

Carolyn: Layers of Pain—PTSD Reaction

Carolyn is a nurturing type of person, the kind of mom whose home is often full of children because she makes her kids' friends feel at home. People gravitate toward her, especially in a crisis, because her gentle spirit calms any atmosphere.

But not so one night when the family was gathered at the kitchen table after dinner. A comment from Carolyn's son, Jeff, triggered an unexpected reaction.

"Can we *not* talk about the fire tonight?" Jeff asked.

Carolyn shot back, "Do you mean the fire that burned EVERYTHING? The fire that erased my memories and stole my safe haven—that fire?"

Something snapped. The F-bomb thundered from her mouth. Louder and louder and louder—at least twenty times, that word shook the air.

Carolyn explained her outburst to me, "How dare anyone not want me to talk about what happened? I couldn't express my feelings after losing everything? I was furious."

The need to survive had hushed Carolyn's voice since early childhood. Now, both the old grief and new pain needed to be expressed and acknowledged by the safe people in her life.

"All the years of stuffing emotions throughout my traumatic childhood exploded out of me. I'd kept quiet long enough.

"The next day, Jeff told me my reaction that night was worse than the fire for him. I would never intentionally hurt my son. I felt bad that I screamed. My reaction frightened me, too."

Anonymous Friend's Story

"I already had PTSD from being in military combat. My symptoms were improving, though. Flashbacks were occurring less often and the nightmares were less frequent. Triggers that had before instantly paralyzed me and caused me to numb out or react were also becoming less frequent.

"Then the fire came....

"The smell of smoke and the sound of crackling embers almost sent me over the edge. I escaped with the clothes on my back and my dog. After the fire, I couldn't move forward; overwhelmed with responsibilities, I froze. The sound of the phone curled me up in a little ball. The mail piled up. I took leave from work....

"Then I got sick, really sick."

What Happens in the Brain to Cause PTSD?

Extreme threat triggers our fight, flight, or freeze mechanisms. As discussed in Chapter 9, the amygdala temporarily shuts off communication to the brain's messaging system so the body can respond to the immediate threat. Blood flows into the large muscles so one can run or fight and all secondary systems, like digestion, halt. This is why when threatened, the heart pounds, palms sweat, and we actually do get tunnel vision. The blood flow has been diverted to the limbs so we can run for our life or fight back. All of our body's resources are focused on survival.

However, when the trauma survivor's coping mechanisms are overwhelmed by trauma and/or remain in a constant state of high alert over an extended period of time, brain injury can occur because the neurological connections are not properly stimulated. When the neurological wires get crossed, the brain no longer knows how to categorize the threat. The brain can't process the memories because the feeling portion of the memory gets stuck in the areas of the brain responsible for logic and vice versa. Because the information isn't processed properly, PTSD can develop.

Support to Heal PTSD

A trained counselor can help calm PTSD symptoms and put the unresolved trauma to rest.

My trauma counselor is an expert in a therapy called Eye Movement Desensitization and Reprocessing (EMDR). According to the EMDR Institute, "The brain's information processing system naturally moves toward mental health. If the system is blocked or imbalanced by the impact of a disturbing event, the emotional wound festers and can cause intense suffering. Once the block is removed, healing resumes."[9]

EMDR therapy advanced my personal recovery. I moved rapidly through rough memories and found peace. Friends of mine also benefitted from this therapy.

The key is to find something that works for you.

The Difference Between Post-Traumatic Stress and Post-Traumatic Stress Disorder

People who have experienced a life-threatening or terrifying event such as a car accident, physical assault, or military combat may experience symptoms of post-traumatic stress such as anxiety, panic attacks, and nightmares. People with post-traumatic stress (PTS) are able to move on and heal after the traumatic event.

With post-traumatic stress disorder, however, memories replay over and over as if the event is happening in real time. "The brain cannot separate 'now and safe' from 'now and danger.'"[10] PTSD is also distinct from PTS because the symptoms persist longer than a month, interfere with daily functions, and get worse instead of better as time passes.

Living With PTSD Symptoms

PTSD manifests differently for each person. Before the fire, I didn't even realize I had PTSD because I generally manage my life well and have healthy relationships. I don't struggle with suicidal thoughts or anger. But some PTSD symptoms had become normal for me—I have had nightmares and flashbacks on a regular basis, although they have become less difficult to deal with over the years.

Whenever my symptoms became too difficult to manage, both before and after the fire, I've sought professional help.

The symptoms most noticeable to my friends have been what I call post-traumatic stress episodes. People close to me have witnessed these episodes at one time or another, such as on the day I lost it in Starbucks. I don't know what triggered that burst of emotion and I couldn't stop it. During these episodes, I couldn't speak because my emotions consumed me. I shook, sobbed, sweated, and felt like I was choking.

Not fun, but it's something I've dealt with since my teen years.

When to Seek Support From a Qualified Professional

- Ideally, within thirty-six hours of witnessing or experiencing a traumatic event
- If you are having suicidal thoughts
- When symptoms are getting worse and not better
- When you feel stuck and are having trouble moving forward
- When having trouble with basic daily functions: eating, sleeping, digesting food, getting out of bed

---

Another manifestation of PTSD has been avoidance. When stressed, I've blocked things out. For instance, when we Manitou Springs residents were allowed to return to our intact homes while the fire was still burning in our area, I felt out of control. I couldn't sit around and do nothing, so I redecorated our living room with the help of an interior designer. We painted my living room and I bought a new couch. Thankfully, my husband put up with me. Looking back, having something to do kept me from dwelling on the disaster around me.

Help is Nearby

When a natural disaster strikes, the Red Cross sets up community centers and makes trauma counselors available. They understand that people may not be aware they need support to work through the crisis. For some, trauma symptoms may show up weeks or months following a disaster.

After the Waldo Canyon fire, trauma affected people in ways they didn't expect. I met dozens who were troubled this way. The saddest scenarios involved people who already had difficult situations to deal with before the additional crisis of the fire's damage. Most of these people retreated and cut off communication with me and others.

It may be that those who isolated themselves have spiraled down to an unhealthy place. Hopefully not.

If you suffer from any PTSD symptoms or have a friend who needs support, I encourage you to find a qualified professional to help. I'm thankful I took the initiative to reach out and receive the guidance I needed. Without support, anxiety can lead to debilitating stress.

Chapter 11

What You Need to
Know About Anxiety

A TRAUMATIC EVENT can unravel the most poised person. Even confident, calm people experience anxiety after a catastrophic event.

For me, anxiety manifested itself in insomnia and nightmares. I was tormented by dreams in which I was attacked, robbed, and raped. The feeling of helplessness also spilled over into dreams in which other people needed help but all I could do was watch them suffer.

I also developed significant anxiety in social situations. I've always been the party planner, the person who loves crowds. But after the fire, I changed. In the early months, crowds overwhelmed me. I hid in restrooms to avoid being with people. I became sensitive to light, noise, and movement. I wanted to be alone in a quiet room.

Not good for someone who works in a people-oriented profession and manages chaos for a living.

How did this happen?

Ann: I Just Need to Know You're There

"I'm not a clingy person. But in the days immediately after the fire, I needed to know where my husband was or I almost panicked. I didn't need to be with him so much as I needed to know I could find him.

"I remember the first week after the fire when we were staying with friends. I asked my friend where Steve was. She said,

'I think he is out in the yard with my husband.' Once I got a glimpse of him, I relaxed. I guess because I lost so much, I was afraid of losing him.

"But gradually, my anxiety tapered away."

Brain Overload Can Cause Sensory Overload

Things that didn't bother people before the fire became overwhelming afterward.

Many of us wondered why crowds made us anxious and irritable. Those of us who normally thrived in an energetic environment yearned for a quiet space away from lights, sounds, and crowds.

What we learned is that trauma increases sensitivity to sensory stimulation.

As explained by Mary Ann Keatley, Ph.D. and Laura L. Whittemore of the Brain Injury Hope Foundation:

> "Any type of trauma, physical or mental, over-sensitizes the brain. Much of the brain's energy is used to filter out irrelevant and unnecessary information. Imagine what it would be like with no filter on your brain. All the sounds, smells, images and feelings would come crashing in at the same time. The overstimulation would probably paralyze you and prevent you from taking any action."[11]

Thus, when the brain is overloaded by stress, little energy is left over for filtering and processing.

Anxiety Can Interfere with Sleep

Eight months after the Cerro Grande Fire, Dr. Barry J. Krakow from Albuquerque, New Mexico, conducted research with seventy-eight fire evacuees seeking treatment for posttraumatic stress sleep disturbances. They were assessed for chronic nightmares, psychophysiological insomnia, and sleep-disordered breathing symptoms.

"My husband and I were both lucky to join the sleep study with Dr. Krakow," Ann said. "He met with anybody who wanted to participate. He asked if we were having recurring nightmares on the same themes."

Both Ann and Steve had been disturbed by nightmares for several months after the fire. Ann's dreams centered on being forced to leave her temporary home. Though her fears were unfounded, "The impermanence of living in a rental home weighed on me," Ann said.

Dr. Krakow recommends, "If you are having a nightmare with a recurring theme, don't dwell on the dreams when you are awake. Think about them enough to recognize the theme and then consciously think of a solution or a different ending."

He gave the example of a woman who dreamed she was being chased to the edge of a cliff. The theme remained the same, but she always woke up before she fell from the cliff. Dr. Krakow gave the lady the same advice he gave us. Several months later, he saw her and asked if she had continued to have the nightmares. "No, your advice worked for me," she said. He asked her what ending she picked for her nightmare. "Oh, I chose to jump."

Ann chose a new ending for her nightmare, too. During the day, she imagined living in a cave on the property where she and Steve planned to build a house. She pictured the cave stocked with everything they needed to feel comfortable. "I thought of this image before I fell asleep at night and the dreams stopped tormenting me."

Anxiety May Manifest as Panic Attacks

Anxiety may also show up as a panic attack. Before the Waldo Canyon fire, most of us had never experienced debilitating anxiety. The unfamiliar symptoms of anxiety scared us and left us with questions that needed answers. For those of us who already had anxiety, the symptoms intensified.

According to the National Institute of Mental Health, anxiety disorders are the most common mental disorder, affecting one in eight Americans between the ages of 18-54. That's nearly 20 million anxious people! The most common anxiety disorder is panic disorder.[12]

Many years ago, I had a panic attack. I was lying on a gurney in pre-op before having hand surgery. Because I had a new baby and wanted to nurse immediately after surgery, I had asked for local anesthesia.

My mind raced as I lay there thinking about being cut open while wide awake. The more I thought about the surgery, the more fearful I became. I felt pressure in my lungs—like I had an elephant sitting on my chest—and had to gasp for air. Suffocating, I called for the doctor. The nurse checked my vitals and reported I was fine.

I certainly was not fine! Why didn't the machines alert them I was dying?

After that, they gave me general anesthesia and I woke up with no breathing problems. I had merely experienced a panic attack.

According to psychologist Bill Gaultiere, Ph.D.:

"It's frightening to experience a panic attack. You feel like you're being smothered and can hardly breathe. Your heart pounds and hurts and you're afraid you're having a heart attack. You tremble or feel tingling or numbness in your hands and feet and you're afraid you're going to faint. You start sweating or have hot and cold flashes. You feel like you're not 'all there;' it all feels so unreal. And worst of all, you're afraid that you're going crazy and that you're going to die!"[13]

How the Body Responds to an Anxiety Attack

Fear and anxiety makes all of the body's energy available to "fight the tiger." Adrenaline pumps blood to the limbs and shuts down blood flow to secondary systems.

The physical sensation of a panic attack is caused by the constriction of blood vessels under the arms and in the pelvic area as the blood is directed to the limbs. Blood vessels in the heart area also constrict, causing a feeling of pressure in the chest and making it difficult to breathe.

What Triggers Panic Attacks?

Panic attacks can be triggered by intense anxiety, as in the situation before my hand surgery. Or they can be triggered by something as simple as the smell of smoke or the sound of a siren.

Some people are triggered by stressful situations such as being in a room full of people, taking a test, or being around certain people. Panic attacks happen with no warning. This is why some people with anxiety are afraid to leave their homes: they fear something will trigger an anxiety attack:

> "Anxiety occurs when you hold the lid down on your pot of boiling emotions," Dr. Gaultiere said. "Eventually, the pressure becomes too great and the lid blows with a panic attack or other anxiety disorder, an angry outburst, or 'acting out' with compulsive behavior (e.g., alcohol, overeating, sex).
>
> Instead of holding the lid down, we need to let off some steam (verbalize our feelings and needs) and turn down the heat (set our limits)."[14]

Panic Attacks Can Happen Even When You're Calm

Months after the fire, while I was lying in bed, I felt pressure on my chest and found it difficult to take a full breath. I felt like the walls were closing in on me. I had exercised earlier in the day, and wasn't feeling any fear or negative emotions.

Why am I having anxiety when I feel completely relaxed? This makes no sense!

My trauma therapy helped me to understand that after your body has been pumped full of adrenaline in a crisis situation like the fire, it eventually needs to purge those toxins. When those by-products of stress are not used, the body will take any chance it can to release them.

So, when we lie down and relax, the body says, "Now is my chance to purge the toxins."

This is another great example of how our bodies are built for health.

How to Stop a Panic Attack

"One surprisingly effective strategy for dealing with a panic attack is to give in. That's right, just let yourself experience it," Gaultiere said. "Instead of fighting, you ride it out while telling yourself, 'I've felt extremely anxious before and it won't kill me.'

"Then start breathing and praying. Or imagine being in a beautiful, peaceful scene. Better yet, fix your thoughts on a comforting Bible passage, like the 23rd Psalm. 'The Lord is my Shepherd, I shall not want...' and imagine the lovely, peaceful scenes."

Important Steps to Take After an Anxiety Attack

Gaultiere explains how to manage the aftermath of an anxiety attack:

"The real key is what you do when you're on the other side of the panic attack. Resolve to find a counselor, pastor, or soul friend who will empathize with you and help you to feel and put words to your distress, fear, anger, sadness, anxiety, and the like. Ask to be listened to and validated. Ask for tender-hearted care.

Along the way, you'll have to deal with some emotional pain and neediness. You'll also have to get to know your Internal Saboteur that sneakily resists or spoils the empathy you need and tells you things like, 'Don't be so emotional... That's weak and needy... You're just going to get hurt... You can't trust people this much... Toughen up and get through this on your own.'

You have to fight off those lies and learn to ask for and accept the grace you need. In the beginning you may need some anti-anxiety medication to re-train your brain,"[15]

With brain training, tools, and support, anxiety can be managed—even when trauma has added another dimension and increased the need for care.

Anxiety after trauma is a normal response to abnormal events. No matter how severe the anxiety, we can heal. Once we understand why we experience anxiety, we have a choice—to endure the effects of trauma or do something about it. This was where many people got stuck following the fires.

In the midst of managing emotional upheaval, the time eventually came for my family and me to excavate the debris from our property.

Before we could clear our lot, though, we needed to sift through the ashes.

Chapter 12

Sifting Through the
Remnants of Our Lives

SIFTING THROUGH THE ASHES and debris of my home mirrored the healing process that was taking place inside of me. The unresolved pain lodged in the closets in my heart needed excavation, too.

That excavation, one step at a time, led to a deeper healing than I knew was possible.

Angels of Mercy

After the initial shock wore off, most families sifted the ashes of their homes, hoping to find meaningful items. The job was backbreaking, dusty, and emotional.

Teams of volunteers, mostly locals, offered to help any family who wanted their assistance. They were coordinated and supported by Samaritan's Purse, a Christian disaster relief organization that provides aid to hurting people around the world.

Our angels of mercy were covered from head to toe in protective white suits, surgical masks, and booties to protect their lungs and skin from the harmful chemicals and asbestos in the ashes. They looked like snowmen, but were sweating in record temperatures of over one hundred degrees.

They shoveled debris over barrels covered with large wire sieves, the kind we used to play with in the sandbox as kids. Working for hours and hours until the job was done, these strangers searched to find remnants of anything that might ease our grief.

Their kindness soothed our open wounds. I felt small next to the goodness they offered.

I chose not to be there on the day Samaritan's Purse worked on my yellow house. The thought of strangers disturbing the ashes unsettled me. I also wanted to give my tenants the space they needed; their belongings had burned, not mine.

But I did visit after the volunteers finished. They had thoroughly searched through the rubble and left everything in order—they'd even swept the driveway. Artifacts were piled on the concrete and garbage barrels were filled with the ashes.

For several weeks afterward, when I drove through my old neighborhood I watched our angels of mercy at work on other ravaged homes. Six weeks after the fire, I met with Bill and Elaine, who told me a heart-warming story about the Samaritan's Purse volunteers.

Bill and Elaine arrived on the property near the end of the sifting job and waited patiently for the Samaritan's Purse team to finish. The team leader of the organization asked Bill and Elaine if the team could pray for them. Bill expressed his hesitancy about praying a Christian prayer because he is Jewish. The leader told Bill he planned to read a Jewish blessing from the Torah.

The leader explained to Bill that while he was praying and planning what to read to the group that morning, he felt compelled to choose the Jewish blessing from the book of Numbers, a book in the Torah. Although he didn't understand at the time, he felt sure these were the words he should pray when they gathered on the property. When he met Bill, he understood.

Bill choked up. The blessing read by the team leader had long been especially meaningful to Bill. It is known to Jews as the Priestly Blessing and is recited by the rabbi while the

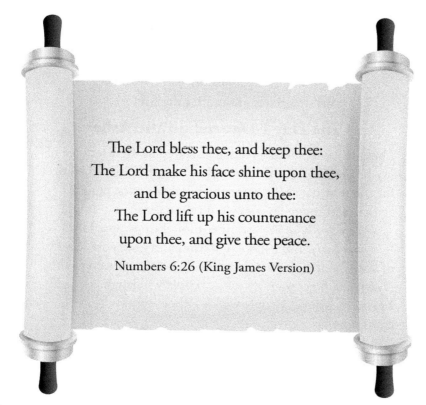

The Lord bless thee, and keep thee:
The Lord make his face shine upon thee,
and be gracious unto thee:
The Lord lift up his countenance
upon thee, and give thee peace.

Numbers 6:26 (King James Version)

congregation is standing. Congregants bow their heads and the rabbi waves his arms as if to enfold them within his (and His) embrace. There is no other prayer like it in the Jewish liturgy.

Touched by the providence of God, the group bowed their heads as the leader prayed over Bill and Elaine.

Along with the special blessing spoken over them, Bill and Elaine recovered their menorah from the rubble, a cherished reminder of faith.

Miraculous Menorah

Journal Entry

August 2012
(two months after the fire)

The Day I Danced on the Ashes

I held my knees to my chest and stared at the wreckage of my burned home. The removal of the ashes was scheduled for the next day. My heart ached, knowing the tangible evidence of my memories would soon settle in a dump.

Dance on the ashes, my quiet thought prompted me.

That's crazy. No. I shook my head and grasped a handful of slate-colored dust—my beautiful house reduced to this.

I'm not dancing on the ashes. People will laugh. I glanced around, people walking their dogs, cars going by.

I am not a singer or a painter, but a dancer. Much had been taken from me, but the expression of my heart remained.

Dance on the ashes. Several times I stood and then sat down, afraid someone would see me.

But my need to proclaim victory over devastation won the argument. I stood, blasted my music, and danced. My inhibitions melted with each step. This was not just a dance, but a simultaneous release of pain and an infusion of strength.

My inner being shouted, *I will overcome. Even if it all burns, I will stand and declare my faith.*

"Great is my God!" The words of the music seared truth into my spirit.

With every step, the broken glass and debris crunched beneath my feet. The sound echoed—a reminder that beauty will triumph, even when brokenness screams.

Sift, Excavate, Remove

Foundations are made to last. Ours didn't.

The intense heat of the fire had destroyed the integrity of our house's concrete and bent the structural steel beams.

After sifting, the next step was excavating and removing all the ashes and debris. Soon, the foundations that once supported our families would be carried to the dump and every lot scraped flat.

Sifting the ashes unsettled me. Excavating them unnerved me. Removal made my loss final. Saying goodbye hurt.

Later the same afternoon, I brought my children back to say our final goodbyes to the ashes and the remnants of our little yellow house.

The sun shone through white marshmallow clouds and soothed our wounds. I had bought five bouquets of flowers, feeling extravagant about spending money on flowers to toss into a hole of rubble, but reminded myself that honoring my loss and saying goodbye was important.

I clutched the flowers in my arms and inhaled their sweet fragrance. My children and I released the rainbow array of flowers. We filled our pile of rubble with blossoms of hope—a promise of a blessed tomorrow.

Letting go of the flowers helped us say goodbye and thank you to the home we loved. I felt courageous. With each flower I tossed, my burden grew lighter.

Making Room for the Future

The excavator explained the process of clearing the lot to me. A tractor scoops the ashes, broken glass, and nails into a plastic-lined dump truck. When the truck is full, the excavating team zips the plastic around the debris like a giant burrito. The driver then unloads the debris at the dump in a spot designated for ashes. Next, a tractor pounds a hole in the foundation wall and crushes the concrete into bits and removes the rest of the debris.

A small lot like mine takes at least four days to clear. Larger lots take from six to twelve days to excavate.

The week they excavated my property, I kept busy to avoid thoughts about the ashes being disturbed. Even though I wasn't physically present, I felt the dust of my memories cloud the sky.

With each layer the tractor extracted, part of me was extracted too.

I was determined, though, to get moving on my rebuild. My lot was one of the first to be cleaned. And ready or not, the rainy season was approaching. Soon, all the leftover debris would become rivers of mush oozing down our streets and into our drainage system.

The rest of the neighborhood *had* to proceed with clearing their lots. City officials sent property owners a formal letter stating that their debris must be removed by a certain date or the city would remove the ashes *for* them—and send the bill.

Though we all needed leadership, some people needed extra time to grieve. I felt sorry for those who were not ready to take action. However, city officials were obliged to encourage our community towards progress and we needed their voice.

Susan: Miracle in the Sea of Impossibility

Susan stood with the Samaritan's Purse volunteers overlooking the ruins of her six-thousand square foot house. A sea of impossibility surrounded the team, yet a gentle voice from one of the volunteers asked, "Is there anything you would like to find?" as if it mattered.

Thinking didn't come easy for Susan because of the overload of stress. But she remembered her soapstone bear from Alaska, a gift. She loved that bear. Saying the words out loud felt pointless as she was certain the bear would never be recovered.

The next day, a member from the team called Susan and asked if the bear was sitting or walking. "Walking," Susan replied.

Later, she was able to tell me, "They found my little bear. Despite a small chip off of his ear and the charring of his little  body, he survived the fire. The team ever-so-proudly presented him to me along with my wedding ring, which they had also recovered."

The bear now sits in the living room of Susan's home, a reminder of small miracles.

Carolyn: New Life

Carolyn welcomed the day they excavated her lot. "I didn't want to see the ruins of my home—I wanted the debris removed from what looked like a war zone."

While the excavation team cleared their lot, Carolyn and her husband watched. They hoped to spot something worth saving under the endless layers of debris, but there was nothing salvageable, only pieces of her childhood doll collection. After days of excavation, their lot was smooth and clean.

Carolyn felt relieved that the painful reminder of her loss was gone. She knew, after living in her house for twenty-two years, nothing would ever be the same. She needed a fresh beginning. Within three weeks, she and her husband signed a contract to build a new home on a lot in another area.

Three years later, a new home was successfully built on their old lot. I love thinking about new life springing up where my old house used to be," Carolyn said.

Deb: Searching Helped Us Say Goodbye

Deb and Denny's family and church friends showed up by the carloads to help them sift their ashes.

People brought ice chests full of drinks and more food than they could eat. Dozens of people, some who they didn't know, worked with them for days in the dusty, clinging, sweaty heat. The kindness of people who cared humbled them. Deb didn't know how to thank everyone who had supported them.

"Our family and friends searched through the ashes, room by room, until certain we had found all we could. They collected six tubs of artifacts; the charred junk seemed like treasure at the time. I couldn't turn my back on the things that might have survived. We honored our past by looking for them. Touching the ashes also gave us a way to say goodbye to all we had lost."

Deb made a Christmas tree out of the burned forks and a lamp out of broken pieces of pottery and glass. "After I had time to heal and put my life back together, I realized the artifacts we collected were nothing more than charred, melted junk. Someday, I may let go of the tubs in my garage. For now, I will keep them."

What disturbed Deb more than sifting the ashes was that she hadn't actually witnessed her home burning. She had left a fully furnished house. When she'd returned, all her belongings were collapsed to almost nothing.

"It would be as if you saw your children as toddlers and the next time you saw them, they were teenagers. If I'd seen my house burn, processing my loss would have been easier."

Ann: People Filled the Void

"There was one thing in particular that we hunted for in our ashes. My husband had a little black bear carved in stone—an unusually well-done medicine bear—which used to sit on a shelf above our bed. We looked in that area but never found the Indian carving my husband treasured. We mentioned the loss of the medicine bear to friends. Many people gave us medicine bears as gifts. Their thoughtfulness helped fill the void of our loss."

When we sifted the ashes of our loss, the search gave us closure. The process helped us comprehend the finality of our loss.

Excavation erased the tangible evidence of our past lives. We had to let go.

Section Three

Rebuilding

Chapter 13

Keys to Surviving Day by Day

RESPONSIBILITIES DON'T CARE about grief—we must keep up with our day-to-day activities.

After the fire, our obligations increased at a time when our hearts and minds demanded significant attention so we could heal. We struggled to balance our responsibilities and our emotional needs. Making it through the day wasn't easy.

Before the crisis, my life moved along like a well-planned play—I showed up and acted my part while the script directed the flow. After the fire, I was forced to act my part while devastated and paralyzed with grief. I wished I could stop the stage from spinning long enough to catch my breath.

Additional obligations resulting from the Waldo Canyon blaze meant working with a new script. Before our house burned, I juggled my responsibilities as wife, mother of two teenagers and four older stepchildren, teacher and church volunteer. After the fire, I also became the decision maker and driver of the rebuild, which required my attendance at an overwhelming number of meetings concerning community and financial issues related to rebuilding.

Rex took care of meals, shopping, and shuttling kids to their activities when he was at home. He also comforted me and provided a safe haven. For him, home is a place to pack and unpack his suitcase. For me, home is the center of everything.

After the fire, the kids and I handled the additional challenges well because of the established structure in our family. Working as a team kept the proper flow of things so we could function.

I put my emotions aside during the day the best I could—allowing any vulnerability interfered with taking care of my job and family. But those quiet hours, mostly late at night and in the early mornings, gave me a chance to pause while I was alone and allow my tears to flow.

I made myself look normal to the casual observer, even in my own home. Sad people can be annoying after a while and I didn't want to drag my family down into my pain.

I often woke up exhausted from processing emotions in the middle of the night. Nevertheless, my concern for my students helped me show up at work each morning. (I taught remedial skills to first through fourth graders in small groups.) When I arrived, I would focus on the sweet faces of my students. They would bounce into my classroom with smiles and eager attitudes.

After my school day, I worked on the rebuild of the house, which was another full-time job. The seemingly endless list of new tasks grew with every contractor meeting and decision made, while I still tried to be a pillar for my family.

If I could make it through the door at work and get started, my job helped push away the cares of the world for a while. But sometimes, a trickle of tears turned into a downpour at the least opportune moments. I hoped if I let them flow I would eventually empty myself of all the tears and pain. The grief counselor from my women's support group always said, "It's better to let the emotion out than to hold it in."

Well, she didn't know my tears had a mind of their own. I wrote the following poem to describe one of those challenging days when I struggled to get started:

Journal Entry

October 2012
(four months after the fire)

Walking Through the Door

Grief stalks me in the quiet hours.
Nights blend into days with little sleep.
While I get ready for work, I wipe my tears
 with my shoulder and keep moving.
On my drive to work, I clear warm streams
 from my cheeks with the backs of my hands.
When I arrive, I gather my things to exit my car.
Time to function, but I'm not ready. I unlock
 the door to the building, inhaling my pain,
 hoping to regain composure.
Enough, I demand. But my tears ignore me.
They know their time is short before I step into
 my teacher role and shut them down.
The more I wipe, the faster the tears pour.
 I walk fast, hoping to shake off my grief.
 I wish I could be invisible.
 My co-worker walks towards me.
 My vulnerability exposed, I burst into sobs.
Embarrassed, I mumble my story through
 those sobs in the hallway of the building.
 The kind man listens.
With a deep breath and a brave posture,
 I walk up the stairs and start my day.

Young Children Are the Best Medicine for a Broken Heart

Each morning when I walked through the common area of the school, the voices of young ones greeted me like a chorus. I felt their loving little arms squeeze my legs. If you haven't been around children, they are transparent and sense vulnerability. They aren't afraid to express the fullness of their emotion, unlike adults who have been warped by growing up and learning to guard their hearts.

I wish my students knew how much those hugs and smiles meant to me all those times I felt fragile.

Keys to Healing

I changed from a survivor to a thriver in the months after the fire because I learned to unlock the tools I needed to heal. Keys come in different shapes and designs to fit our unique style of grieving. Learning what fits for you is part of the journey of healing.

We Need People

Feeling understood is the one pain medicine that soothes the deepest wounds.

Connections to others were one of my keys. Like the co-worker who listened to me in the hallway, the kindness of others kept me moving. Lovely people gave me a boost when grief threatened my ability to function.

Sitting eye to eye, heart to heart, with someone who "gets" your pain is worth a thousand hours of therapy. We all need at least one person who understands us.

A publication about healing the effects of trauma states, "We need others to listen to us, to validate the importance of what happened to us, to bear witness, and to understand the role of this trauma in our lives."[16]

We all grieve differently. Some people need to find connections right away by getting involved in community activities or spending time with friends. Crisis draws out our vulnerability, which gives us the opportunity to start new relationships while deepening the ones we already have.

Trauma causes others to retreat and isolate. Those people need time by themselves to process emotions before they will be ready to reach out or join a support group. If this sounds like you, give yourself permission to take a breath and acknowledge it is okay to reach out when you are ready. Building a larger support community can take place after the initial shock wears off.

Routine Activities Can Be Stabilizing

After the fire, routine activities became stabilizing anchors we could depend upon while we worked through the trauma. Our workplaces provided a familiar environment untouched by the fire and our jobs became a positive distraction.

Those residents who worked out of their homes suffered an additional layer of trauma because they couldn't escape to a stable workplace. An artist from my support group lost her home art studio as well as thousands of dollars' worth of her artwork to the fire. There was no way to replace the stacks of art, representing hundreds of hours of work. Her rental policy paid pennies on the dollar—nowhere near the value of her loss. She had to start over.

Each of us pushed on, putting one foot in front of the other and trudging the path ahead of us. Most of us felt more settled once we knew where we were going to sleep and what we were going to do each day. The sooner we settled into a routine, the better.

Even a routine as simple as eating the same breakfast each day provided an anchor of security. For me, I looked forward to my Starbucks coffee in the morning. A raspberry mocha-nonfat-extra hot-half the syrup with whipped cream cup of coffee may have saved me from cracking. I figured going through the drive-thru for coffee each day cost less than getting admitted to a hospital. Simple, but true—that cup of coffee gave me incentive to keep moving.

I learned, through trauma, to respect people's vices when they are in a crisis. I'm much less judgmental now when I see someone with a bad habit.

Do One Thing You Enjoy Every Day

I made it a point to do one special thing for myself every day.

Being in nature revives me, so I would take a walk or drive to a creek to sit by the water. I'd even give myself permission to lie down for a few minutes and listen to music, even though the laundry was piled up and dinner needed to be cooked. At work, I often made it a game to see how far and fast I could walk during my lunch break. Making it around our small town in fifteen minutes gave me a sense of satisfaction.

Say Yes to Support

A giver often has trouble receiving.

The people of the affluent Mountain Shadows area were used to giving to others in need. But when they became homeless, many felt awkward being on the receiving end. One lady from my cul-de-sac had always been the first person to show up with a casserole when a neighbor had a death in the family. She had volunteered at the homeless shelter and served food there once a month. After the fire, she herself was suddenly homeless.

Friends and family offered to bring her clothes and supplies. She declined, "Thanks, anyway, but I'm fine."

The truth is, nobody is fine after a fire destroys their home.

This kind lady needed support but didn't know how to receive it. "So many people are worse off than me," she said.

We needed to understand that people cared about us and wanted to help. When we hurt, others also hurt for us. When my friend and co-worker, Donna, went through her own traumas, she didn't want to accept support. At first, she didn't think she needed it.

But she learned that helping is for others, too. Donna said, "Let people support you, even if you don't feel like you need it. Those who give to you gain something from their giving."

Allow People to Help You Prioritize

We may not know what we need after trauma.

Kristin told me about the day she went to Kohl's department store with a friend who came to help her.

Her friend asked, "What do you need?" The question overwhelmed Kristin. She couldn't answer at first.

At last she blurted, "Socks and underwear. If my kids have socks and underwear they will be fine."

"Okay," her friend said, and they filled the basket together.

Kristin needed so much more, but in that moment, she could only focus on socks and underwear.

Advice from others can help us prioritize at a time when we can't think clearly. A friend or a counselor can sit with us and help us focus.

Let People Know What You Need

Friends and loved ones want to support us, but they may not know how. If we come up with a few ideas ahead of time, we will be able to respond when asked.

Consider making a list of items for people to buy or suggest gift cards. Also, make a list of those services people could do, like watching your children or inviting you for a home-cooked meal. Think about what is helpful and what isn't.

When you have a better idea of the ways others can support you, send out an email. Let them know you may not be able to respond to phone calls and emails for a time, but you would really appreciate hearing from them. (You could also ask a friend to be your contact person and send updates on your behalf.)

When we take responsibility for what we ask for, we can gratefully receive as well as avoid frustration when people unknowingly respond in a way that is not helpful.

Journaling

Christie Lee, my trauma counselor, encourages her patients to journal because writing releases built-up psychological energy. I have found this to be very true. I feel a sense of control when I capture the intensity of my emotion in writing. The paper I write on becomes a witness to my grief and helps me let it go. Journaling gives thoughts and emotions permission to flow.

Find Positive Distractions

Christie Lee explained that positive activity distracts us from our pain and literally creates healthy new neural pathways in the brain. Focusing on pleasurable activity "resets" the brain, effectively shifting our emotional gears to maneuver out of the mud of our negative emotions.

When I had insomnia, spending time on creative websites helped calm my mind and, eventually, helped me sleep. Pinterest and Houzz were places where I could think about things other than the upheaval in my life.

Pinterest is a website designed to construct collages of peoples' favorite things. I organized collages that were meaningful to me—animals, quotes, favorite books, recipes, etc. Houzz.com gave me creative ideas for home design—dreaming about the details of my new house refocused me. When I searched my areas of interest online, I connected to my essence, the part of me that needed to focus on something normal.

Positive distractions also helped Donna and her husband, Rick, deal gracefully with traumatic situations over many years. So when they talk, I listen.

Donna is a survivor of a double mastectomy and Rick is her saintly support. After the stress of battling cancer, their son's house burned down. Two granddaughters and a grandson died in the fire. This would be enough trauma for anyone to bear in a lifetime. Then the situation worsened—their son was accused of arson and causing the death of his three children. Two years later, their son was arrested, went to trial, and was imprisoned. Donna and Rick continue to battle the appeal process in hopes their son will be released. "His incarceration was a travesty. Our flawed court system failed us. We wait patiently for good news," Donna said.

"You can't let your grief drag you down." Donna said. "If you think about your loss all the time you can't move forward. You have to find something to distract yourself."

Sometimes You Need to Laugh

Immediately after the fire, Kristin purchased replacement items for her family of five. She struggled to remember what the new things looked like.

Two months after the fire, Kristin watched her child's team play soccer. When practice ended, she bagged her chair, grabbed her camera, and started walking.

A man walked up to her and said, "Can I help you?"

"No thanks, the game is over and we're going now."

"Where are you going with my things?"

She apologized profusely, mortified she had inadvertently walked off with the man's stuff. With all their new possessions, keeping track of everything was a challenge. Kristin and I laughed when she remembered this incident. In situations like this, humor gives us a much-needed break from the stress.

Have Something to Look Forward To

I think we are strong enough to do just about anything if we know there will be a reprieve or an end to our hardship. Looking forward to a future event can lift our spirits when circumstances exhaust and consume us.

For a whole year after the fire, I dreamed about staying at The Castle. On particularly difficult days, I said to myself, "Soon, I will have my retreat at The Castle."

The Castle at Glen Eyrie is one of my favorite places and dear to my heart. I married Rex there. This retreat center and hotel is nestled in the mountains of Colorado Springs and filled with gardens and beautiful places to absorb nature. The thought of going to this special place kept me moving during many hard days.

After the first anniversary of the fire, I kept my promise to myself and checked into The Castle. (My husband lives in hotels seventeen days a month and has no desire to spend time in another one.) As it turned out, Rex was away that weekend anyway, the kids were busy, and The Castle had an available room—as if saved just for me. The sounds of happy birds and the creek flowing beneath my window welcomed me. I wandered through the marvelous gardens and hiked up the mountain paths, soaking in the rare gift of quiet time alone. My one-night stay gave me the reprieve I had dreamed of.

I also dreamed about the day when my new home would be finished. I planned a party in my imagination to celebrate that day, envisioning a gathering of the friends who had helped me rebuild. The thought of inviting all the people who had helped me along the way to celebrate the completion of the house kept me going.

As it happened, when the house was completed after seven months of construction, it didn't work out for me to have a party. By then, I had thanked people in my own way and didn't need a party to express my gratitude. Still, creating the party in my imagination gave me something to look forward to and helped me in my recovery process.

Remember: Tomorrow Is a New Day

Donna and Rick said, "Whatever you are going through, remember that tomorrow is a new day. Our loss is always going to be there. Time doesn't heal our wounds, but it does lessen the pain." The sun goes down on every bad day and closes the curtain on the pain of yesterday. Each morning the sun rises with a promise of a better day.

Hope drew us to move on and overcome our calamity.

To overcome, though, we needed to feel safe.

Chapter 14

How to Find Your Safe Place

TRAUMA HAD SHAKEN the very foundation of our community.

Many of us felt helpless, hopeless, and hapless. We all needed to feel secure, to regain balance, to stand strong again.

Many people didn't realize that a great deal of their anxiety stemmed from feeling terribly vulnerable. When they learned that anxiety is a normal response to trauma and they needed safe places to help them recover, those safe places became easier to find.

I struggled to understand why my loss had traumatized me more than many others in my community. Some people appeared to brush off the dust of devastation and move on without looking back. Others, like me, unraveled and needed more support to heal.

Through a process of reflection and gaining knowledge, I learned why the destruction of my house had affected me so dramatically: My safe place had burned.

Safety is more than a physical space—it's a feeling. When I saw my devastated house, buried emotions shredded my heart like flying shrapnel. All at once, the forces of childhood memories and trauma shattered my well-put-together life and I was a vulnerable little girl, curled up in a ball, lying in the broken pieces of my past.

Alcoholism, broken families, and violence had hurt me deeply from my earliest years. My dad starting drinking when he was nineteen years old, unaware that his first beer would lead to decades of heartache and chaos. My parents divorced when I was five. Dad remarried and divorced several times. My mom remarried a man I adored, but his drinking caused deep emotional scars and led to the domestic violence that forced my mom, sister, and me to flee when I was thirteen.

I thought I had recovered. I thought I had worked through those sad events, forgiven others and myself, moved on. But everything I had tried to mend felt undone. I was raw, vulnerable, unsafe.

My yellow house had been one of my safe places. Now, its ashes were a physical place where I could let down my guard. I sat at the gravesite of my burned house more frequently than I would like to admit. The ashes comforted me because they held my memories—they bore witness to my life in the house.

Nobody outside my immediate family knew my history. But my house did. If my house could talk, it would tell about all the memories that have blurred with time. If it had eyes, it would replay the sweetest movies of my toddlers (now teenagers), showing details I don't remember and moments I don't want to forget. It would hear our laughter and feel the warmth of our love.

The ashes understood what others couldn't. I didn't have to explain what I had lost. What had been walls with history were now ash in my hands, but it was still mine. Though I spent time there regularly, my family didn't—at least not the way I did. They did respect my need and supported me.

Working with my trauma counselor helped me to understand why the catastrophic event of the Waldo Canyon fire caused my painful past to resurface. With her assistance, I learned to establish physical and emotional safe places, so I could walk through more recent injuries that needed attention.

The rubble of my yellow house became my place to grieve. I would come with a heavy heart and always felt lighter by the time I left. On days when I felt particularly downcast, animals would visit me. A mother deer with her fawns would nibble her way near me or a massive buck would present himself. They seemed to know I needed them.

Magical moments continually surprised and delighted me during my visits. A few months after the fire, I sat cross-legged on the driveway. A grey rabbit hopped close to me. At first, I thought I'd frightened him and he was trying to make himself invisible. I moved closer, thinking he would hop away. Instead, he stared at me and stood on his hind legs. The furry little creature addressed me with calmness and seemed to say, "All things will be beautiful in time. Life and beauty will remain."

Many "rabbits" spoke to me during my journey of healing. The gravesite of my burned yellow house was transformed into a beautiful house as the months progressed.

At each stage of rebuilding, I felt safe there.

Carolyn: New Home Became New Safe Space

Many other families lost their safe places, too. Home was a refuge from life's difficulties—the place to relax. Carolyn described the significance of her home being her safe haven. "Coming home at night and sitting in that special spot on my sofa with my little pillows meant a lot, since I didn't grow up in a safe place."

After losing her home, Carolyn struggled to recreate a safe space. She went from living in a beautiful 4,000 square foot home to living at a friend's house with all of her worldly possessions in a cardboard box. "We had several temporary living spaces but I did not have my own comfortable space. I had no anchor. I didn't feel safe.

"I had to learn to let go of the things I had lost—the history of my life, all of the trip memorabilia, even my tangible memories, and realize I would be okay. I learned that my security is within me. I believed I would make it through this trauma and thrive again. Recovery was a huge process.

"When our new home was built, I felt apprehensive about moving in because our temporary home had become our safe place for a year and a half. Even though we would be moving into a new, beautiful house, I didn't want to move. Change unsettled me. I told myself, *You can do it. Just get up and go.* Once we moved in, we loved our new home."

Through the willingness to examine her feelings, Carolyn not only recreated a safe place in her new home, she also learned to become her own safe haven. She found a new kind of peace within herself she hadn't had before the fire.

A Community Can Be a Safe Place

People I met because of the fire became a nurturing community for me.

Beth worked at the flooring store where I picked out materials for my home. She spent hours with me choosing tile, hardwood, and carpet. She had also lost her home in the Mountain Shadows neighborhood, so we identified with each other. I looked forward to our appointments together. Every time we met, we felt like long-time friends, even though our only connection was our common crisis.

Johnny Wilson was another person who became part of my community. He was one of the people who listened to my story—not only with his ears, but with his heart. He took photos of over one hundred fire victims and created a book with their hand-written stories. When I came to his studio for my photo, I'll never forget the way he treated me. He listened to my story as if understanding my pain was the only thing that mattered. Knowing Johnny cared brought aid to the part of me that felt alone. People like Beth and Johnny fueled my healing.

Kristin: People With the Same Experiences Can Be a Safe Place

Kristin, her husband Doug, and their three children (a first grader, fifth grader, and seventh grader) forged ahead with support from their community members. Their openness encouraged their own healing process and that of others, too.

Working as a middle school teacher brought Kristin a sense of purpose as she served people who had been affected by the fire.

Kristin bonded with her students in a most unusual way. "After my husband left for work and I was teaching my students, my job was a reprieve from everything," she said. "There were other teachers and students who had also lost their homes, which made the stress more manageable.

"Often, I would have a student say, 'I would have stapled this, but I don't have a stapler.' Or, 'I couldn't print my assignment because we don't have a printer yet.' They would say, 'I didn't get my homework done because we were doing house stuff.' I would say, 'I get it, just take another day.' I had a special sensitivity with the students because I understood the stresses they were under."

At work, Kristin identified with the people who shared her experience. Together, her students and co-workers journeyed through the process of rebuilding.

Thomas: Living in a Different World

In contrast, Thomas worked in an area unaffected by the fire. Even though his coworkers lived in Colorado Springs, many of them didn't realize the magnitude of the event that had taken place across Waldo Canyon, just a few miles away.

Thomas' workplace was in downtown Colorado Springs, fifteen minutes from the remains of 347 homes. His work resumed immediately after the fire, as if nothing had happened. The burned area wasn't even visible from his office, as it was blocked by a mountain ridge.

"My co-workers weren't involved in what I experienced," Thomas said. "The office felt like another world. I had experienced a horrific event, but the rest of the staff hadn't been personally affected by the fire."

However his neighbors, family, and friends kept him going. "Dozens of people contacted me: old friends, friends from church, people I had forgotten about. People cared. Their support meant so much to me."

A Support Group Can Be a Safe Place

My women's support group provided a safe place to process my emotions. Women who shared a common experience and were grieving the same loss welcomed me. Instantly, the group felt safe and became a refuge for me. This was one place where our vulnerabilities could surface after toughing it out during the week.

We supported each other. When I had to miss a meeting due to family obligations, I found comfort in knowing the group was together. I felt like they were there for me, even when I couldn't make it to the meeting.

We had become each other's safe place. We didn't have to explain what we'd gone through.

Our support group was one place where we didn't have to gear up for an accidental assault: at times, well-meaning people would accidentally say horrible things because they didn't understand our pain. For instance, neighbors whose homes hadn't burned became frustrated because they had to look at their neighbors' debris. "When do you think this mess is going to get cleaned up?"

Their words hurt. We needed time to work on our property and dispose of the remnants of our precious memories. When our group discussed comments like this, we processed our experiences together. Building a support community may be awkward at first, but it is worth the effort.

A Person Can Be a Safe Place

I remember, as a child, sitting on my grandma's lap when she was in her rocking chair. I can still hear the sound of the back and forth vibration from the worn-out rocker. Grandma's arms holding me kept the cares of the world away.

Safe people help us feel comfortable enough to let down our guard.

My husband was (and is) a safe person for me. He listened and allowed me to share the details of my grief without trying to fix it. My trauma counselor also helped me feel safe. Christie Lee understood how the trauma had impacted me and put into words those things I couldn't explain. She helped me to make sense of my feelings and move forward. I had gone through a traumatic experience, suffered loss, and needed validation.

I needed to spend time with safe people who tried to understand me. Safe people say things such as, "Help me understand what you are going through" or, "I can only imagine how much pain you are feeling."

Some people couldn't relate to our experience and inadvertently harmed us when we were vulnerable. My neighbor went to her doctor because she couldn't sleep after her house burned down. The doctor told her, "Have a cup of tea and get over it." We are fragile, we have to guard our hearts.

I avoided sharing with people who had responded earlier with statements such as, "That wasn't so bad," "You have dwelled on this long enough," or, "If you think that's bad, let me tell you what happened to me." I only had so much energy, so I spent time mostly with people who could support me.

Well-meaning folks may not know how to be a safe person. However, if a relationship is important, we can teach them how to help us.

Doing Something Significant Can Be a Safe Place

Doing something positive can give us a sense of control when we are devastated.

Some people are naturally take-charge problem solvers. They are the leaders who create structure for others. They led our community in rebuilding, even though they had lost their homes too.

These fine people endured disaster and used their abilities and energy to take control for the safety and good of all the rest. These courageous men and women became pillars for those who were floundering and frozen in grief.

My way of taking control in a helpless situation was to focus on restoration.

The impact of the destruction dazed my neighbors. When I spoke to them about rebuilding their homes, they looked at me with blank stares, unable to visualize anything other than the surrounding devastation. I hoped that if my neighbors saw new construction arise from the ashes, they would also have the courage to move forward. So, three months after the fire, the foundation of my house was one of the first to resurrect from the rubble.

My friends Carolyn and Susan M. also made a significant difference by organizing my support group, the Wonderful Waldo Women. Though Carolyn wasn't a formal leader, I relied on her for leadership. Her willingness to lead the meetings and share her vulnerability helped all of us. She set the atmosphere for us to give ourselves permission to fall apart when we needed to.

The ladies were *wonderful* because the grace and support shared in this group was rare. Seldom do you find a group of women who turn their grief into the power to heal each other. Bonds of camaraderie built friendships.

When the Black Forest fire raged in the Colorado Springs

Journal Entry

October 2012
(four months after the fire)

Eating Lunch in the Dark

Everything I did required more effort than under
normal circumstances. I had limited capacity for
small talk. Even breathing took effort, so I needed
a few minutes of solitude from the full classrooms
and busy halls.

The school building where I worked, built in
1923, echoed with children's voices and footsteps
on the hardwood floors. I searched the building for
a reprieve from the chatter and found the perfect
spot in the dark balcony of the auditorium.

I climbed the wooden stairs and sank into a
squeaky chair, making myself invisible and quiet.
Lunches in the dark comforted me as I focused on
being still and nurturing the part of myself that
needed a quiet place.

area, less than a year after the Waldo fire, the Wonderful Waldo Women organized support for the new fire victims. Their strength and concern for others astounded me. Five years after the fire, the Wonderful Waldo Women still meet, thanks to the two women who ventured to start a much-needed support group.

Solitude Can Be a Safe Place

People assumed I ought to be fine because the house I lost was my second home. For the most part, my co-workers were unaware of how much the crisis affected me because the town where I taught didn't burn. Plus, I tried to look normal on the outside to avoid emotions so I wouldn't fall apart.

But inside, grief wanted to swallow up my soul, it seemed, and lingering stresses threatened to become all-absorbing. It was all I could do to save my energy and to stay focused at work. Though I needed support from others, I also needed time alone to sort out my emotions. At lunch, I would disappear into my quiet place where I could refocus and recharge.

Before the fire, I enjoyed community activities. After the crisis, social events overwhelmed me.

I couldn't go to church. I tried, but I couldn't. Though people in church were supportive of me, the area around our church hadn't been directly affected by the fire. Parishioners didn't understand what we were going through. Also, huddling together inside a building seemed wrong when others outside the building needed so much.

Moreover, I didn't have the energy to express to the church folks what I had been through. What I needed more was simply time alone to process my feelings. So I sent my family to church without me for several months while I had my own private church services at the charred foundation of our yellow house. I sat with God, a cup of coffee, and solitude. Being quiet there was the necessary thing to do for a period of time.

Thomas: Gratitude Knits Communities Together

Thomas used his leadership skills to bring people together.

He and his neighborhood organized a barbecue to honor the firemen and police officers who fought the Waldo Canyon fire. He contacted all the fire departments involved and the fire chief. Even a deputy chief came to the event.

"We blocked off the street and celebrated the service of our first responders," Thomas said. "My neighborhood worked together to make this happen. Doing something positive was my way of dealing with the horrific event."

Faith Can Be a Safe Place

Whether they had a particular faith or no faith at all, people asked tough questions:

Why did God allow this to happen? Why? Why have I been abandoned? How will I recover? What am I supposed to learn from this? Why is the house next door standing and mine is gone? Does God like them and not us? Then, *Why not me?*

We didn't have the answers, but we did have each other.

Friends of mine, who aren't church-going people, attended events sponsored by various churches, such as First Presbyterian in downtown Colorado Springs. That church welcomed all affected by the fire. Members of the church organized grief groups and welcomed everyone, regardless of faith differences. Churches provided a supportive place for anyone who wanted one.

There were also faith groups that poured out gifts and kindness with love. Samaritan's Purse showed up to serve wounded people. They didn't preach and asked for nothing in return.

Many people who believed in God tucked their loss and sorrow into their faith. They had a structure to cling to, a church to attend, the Bible to read, and a history of answered prayers to reflect upon. Others without a religious faith clung to family and friends, and their beliefs.

Our earthly possessions and comforts had burned and left us with what we had inside—our core. Faith or no faith, people shared what they had.

Deb: Our Faith Kept Us Strong

"In the face of disaster, we never questioned our faith. It was there, right there beside us, to hold onto and keep us strong. I'm thankful we had grown strong in the Lord before the fire happened. We knew God would always be there for us. We never shed a tear. My husband joked that at least he didn't need to clean out the garage anymore and he was glad to have new underwear. Over time, we replaced our household items, but I no longer feel attached to 'stuff' and happily give it away. I am free, which in turn makes me rejoice over my loss."

Donna and Rick: We Gave Ourselves Permission to Grieve

Donna and Rick found a safe place in each other and in their faith. "We gave ourselves permission to feel sad and get angry at the world, other people, and, particularly, ourselves," Donna said. "Once we expressed our feelings, we prayed and counseled with our pastor, who was a great support and spent hours upon hours with us. We learned we are not in control and we can only give everything to the Lord.

To make it through the day, we gave our situation to the Lord hourly and, frequently, moment by moment. Having faith has certainly helped us."

Finding ways to feel safe after a traumatic experience like a fire takes time, effort, and support. When we find safe places, it's important to give ourselves permission to spend time in those places and with those people so we can process our grief.

Once we had a sense of safety, healing required removing layers of debris both from our hearts and our damaged property. To restore our homes and heal emotionally, we needed to sift through the damage and excavate what didn't belong.

For me, the trauma from the fire became the catalyst to open the closed closets in my heart. To open those doors, I needed to look back before I could move forward.

Chapter 15

Look Back Before You Look Forward

FOR MONTHS AFTER THE FIRE, I had insomnia. When I did sleep, horrific nightmares were worse than not sleeping. My food wouldn't digest. Routine tasks became difficult. Instead of getting better, my distress intensified.

At this point, I stopped fighting grief because I had no choice. This time in my life presented an opportunity for deep cleansing. I submitted.

Emotion consumed me, mostly when I tried to sleep. When I was able to pour out my raw feelings on paper, I could let them go and put them to rest. The journal entry on the next page helped me express my emotions one sleepless night.

New Wounds Healed Old Scars

The fire leveled my house—and me.

Stripped of my defenses, I felt vulnerable and exposed.

The sudden ruin of my home and neighborhood occurred when I was an adult, a mirror of the devastating losses of my childhood. It also exposed the raw emotions I had felt as a child but hadn't known how to express.

Through my work with Christie Lee, I came to understand my feelings of hopelessness, helplessness, and haplessness in reaction to the fire were the same as those I felt in my youth. Thus, my past hurts became part of my present trauma.

When I was thirteen, life as I knew it disappeared overnight when my mom removed my sister and me from our home

Journal Entry

August 20, 2012
(two months after the fire)

Rubble Beneath my Feet

I can't escape the ache in my heart. Pain is swelling in my chest. God, help me excavate the darkness.

Tonight I feel ashes and broken pieces of loss beneath my bare feet where my house once stood. Jagged edges of ruin press the emptiness. The ashes wail a gut-wrenching cry. They sing out of anguish, for not just the loss of a home, but for all the losses of my life—each singing their own notes.

because of domestic violence. We never returned. And no one talked about why we left because people didn't talk about abuse back then. We fled to a hotel and later moved into a rental house in the same town.

Our losses were catastrophic—our affluent lifestyle in the country, surrounded by beautiful trees and our pets, disappeared over night. We went from ski vacations at the best resorts to worrying about turning on the heat because the bill would cost too much. I lost living next door to my best friend, Marissa. In a sense, I lost my mom, too. She had been a stay-at-home mother, but leaving forced her to work long hours. We did our best to adjust.

With the coming of the great fire, all my early losses were resurrected and demanded attention. I found myself in trauma counseling, pouring out feelings from my childhood long ago. My emotions felt raw, as if I was a teenage girl experiencing those feelings for the first time.

Old issues re-emerged in other people as well. After surveying the external damage to their homes, some encountered internal damage from their pasts. Like me, they thought their wounds were healed, their work was done. We wondered why past hurts from divorce, lack of security, or loss of a loved one had re-emerged.

The grief counselor from my women's support group assured us, "After a traumatic event, it's normal for past trauma to re-emerge. Trauma triggers past feelings of vulnerability."

Carolyn: Losing My Safe Place Revealed Old Scars

The fire's destruction triggered past trauma from Carolyn's childhood.

"I felt like a little orphan girl when the house I had built and lived in for over twenty-two years was gone. If someone had grown up with a normal upbringing, I'm not sure if losing his or her home in a fire would have had so much meaning.

"When I got married, I built the home I never had. I made it a priority to create a safe place for my children because my parents had neglected me in my childhood. Losing the home I had created for my safe haven made me lose my safety and security all over again. My home was more than a structure, it was my new life after being traumatized as a child—my nest.

"As a kid, I didn't have proper nurturing. Growing up was like living in a war zone. My mom was a battered wife. Dad came home after drinking and we were emotionally and sometimes physically battered. It wasn't just mom—it was us kids, too.

"I had no structure and no routine. We didn't have set times for meals or family dinners. I'd go to friends' homes and hope they would ask me to stay for dinner. We had to grow up really fast and do most everything for ourselves.

"I remember when Mountain Chalet, a local store, gave away a pair of shoes to those Mountain Shadows residents who had lost their homes. I put on the shoes and regressed to being a little girl again. I started crying because I never had anything new as a child. I used to get everyone's hand-me-downs. Every time someone gave me something I didn't have after the fire, I felt those vulnerable feelings all over again."

Trauma Broke Down My Barriers

The image of my home burned to rubble symbolized the crumbled wall of protection I had built around my heart to survive. I needed to be tough as a kid because of family challenges and other wounds accumulated in my youth.

But after the fire, I didn't have enough energy to guard my heart. Years of built-up defenses crumbled with my house.

Reliving my former helplessness brought me to the most vulnerable places in my being. The fire demanded a deep cleansing, like a forest fire cleanses the land and makes it stronger. I, too, will be stronger.

I wrote the poem on the next page to describe the wall I had built to protect myself.

Walls Can Protect Us or Harm Us

Lowering my defenses felt good. I didn't realize how much energy it took to carry my armor. My wall kept bad stuff out, but it also kept good stuff from coming in.

Guarding my heart is important, but not at the expense of being known by the people who love me.

Carolyn also felt relieved to let down her defenses after learning to protect herself in her youth. Her tears, triggered by the loss of her home, washed away years of unresolved emotion she didn't know she had.

Carolyn: Behind My Wall of Tears

"When I was a child, I had to be strong to survive. I couldn't break down and be a weak little girl. I had to be tough. I don't cry easily. I am still not one of those people who can cry at the drop of a hat.

"After the fire, though, my safe place had been ripped out from under me. Unlike some people, I could not stop crying. My vulnerability was exposed and I broke wide open. The egg cracked and I couldn't stop crying.

"For the first time in my life, emotion really poured out of me. It felt good to cry hard after locking in my hurt all of my life. I love crying now because I had never allowed myself to cry before. I was used to being tough. During this time, when my tears flowed I thought, 'Bring it on!'

Journal Entry

January 16, 2012
(seven months after the fire)

The Wall

Curiosity drew me to the wall
Familiarity drew me closer
A fog of pain encapsulated me
Warmth from my touch
   made the wall transparent
This was my wall, formed
   with each wound,
Built by a need for protection
The mortar solidified by my tears
My faces from the past illuminated
   from inside,
Faces of pain worthy of memorializing
Each face etched in the stone
beckoned acknowledgement
Many faces cried out to me,
Reminding me that ignoring their
   presence would not make them
   go away
Some stood out more than others
   calling me to set them free

"In time, however, my discovered vulnerability started to close up and I couldn't access my tears anymore. Something has to hit me just right at a certain core level for me to be able to cry."

Pain Reminds Us We Are Not Healed

Our physical bodies mirror the emotional process of healing. Injuries make us weak and vulnerable at the site of the injury.

When I was a kid, I tore the ligaments in my knee while skiing. For years, the slightest bit of stress aggravated my injury. When the weather got cold, my knee felt achy and stiff. The ache reminded me that the damage wasn't completely healed. I massaged my knee and applied heat during each bout of discomfort. After about seven years, my discomfort gradually faded.

As with physical injuries, emotional pain is a reminder to slow down and pay attention. Trauma can reveal to us the most vulnerable wounds in our hearts and give them voice.

"Traumatized people do far better in therapy because their emotions aren't guarded," Dr. Rudy said. "From a spiritual standpoint, we are designed for wholeness. Loss and trauma provide an opportunity to let go of the extra baggage on the inside that makes us unhealthy. The Lord doesn't want to take things away from us, except for the unhealthy stuff on the inside that isn't good for us. Trauma provides an opportunity to empty unhealthy baggage that harms us so we can reach our full potential and fulfill our purpose."

Moving Forward: I Am Vulnerable, Now What?

Like in the poem, *The Wall*, ignoring wounds doesn't make them go away.

The fire stripped my defenses. I could have ignored issues that came up, but I didn't want to risk them popping up later uninvited. I chose to do the necessary work to heal. I received support from others instead of isolating within myself. I also took the time I needed to process my experience alone.

We each process loss in different ways. Some of us need to take more time to work through painful issues. Each of us sets our own pace and chooses the depth of our healing process.

The grieving process itself, though, is similar in most cases, regardless of the loss. I'm inspired by my friends Donna and Rick. In light of everything they have lived through, their positive attitude and ability to show up at work with a smile inspires me. I asked them what advice they would give to others going through trauma and loss.

"Share your grief with others. Don't keep it inside. Stuffing the pain will make it worse. Find a grief group, because you will need support to deal with a major loss. We are people who just move forward, but we learned to pause so we could heal. Our grief class showed us we had not dealt with everything in our past. Grieving past losses along with present losses helped us heal."

Donna and Rick's words encouraged me. Healing required trudging through the debris—present and past. I embraced the challenge of confronting old wounds, which led to pleasant surprises.

Chapter 16

I Vowed Not to Waste My Pain

GRIEVING IS FOR THE COURAGEOUS.

Waves of grief can pull us under—or we can ride them. Whether they are tidal waves or gentle swells, far apart or close together, we can't avoid their impact. If we run, grief will overtake us. If we try to contain grief, it will overflow.

I witnessed hundreds of people in my community grieve—like different types of music, each had their own song to express their grief. Some clung to their faith and loved ones. Others expressed grief through anger, silence, depression, denial, numbness, isolation, physical ailments, avoidance through busyness, and combinations of all these coping strategies.

The aftermath of mass destruction helped me to form a deeper level of respect for grieving people.

Doing the Work to Heal

With the walls that had guarded my heart torn down and a support system in place, I allowed myself to grieve old losses that still affected me.

Emotions corked up for decades splattered on my tranquil life. I vowed not to waste any of my pain. I wanted the emotional upheaval caused by the fire to really count.

I'm a get-the-job-done, full-speed-ahead kind of person. But the fire—it had power and slowed me down. Thus, my vulnerability surfaced and gave me the opportunity to heal at a deeper level than I had in my younger years. In my youth,

Journal Entry

September 27, 2012
(three months after the fire)

The Valley I Wondered About

The valley…
So, this is the valley of the shadow of death.
I'm not dead, but I feel death.
Jesus must be with me. I know because I would
    suffocate without His presence.

Pain swallows my breath to the faintest flow,
A fog of death descends on every cell in my body.
Groans of anguish stab my senses,
From pits of emptiness, crushed souls wail
    songs of sorrow.

I have wondered about this valley…now I know.
This is the place where the broken people come,
    I am not alone.
Weights of grief push the light from me,
The ache squelches the beauty
    from all good things.

I refuse to stay here. But, I must walk through.
I am here to replace lies with truth.

Others are here because they have lost someone.
Grief paralyzes them. They can't find their way out.

Good Shepherd, don't let me leave until I am
    healed and restored.
Remove all of us broken people from this place.

traumatic events had overwhelmed me. I didn't have the maturity or tools to process all the facts and feelings surrounding each loss. As an adult, my work with my trauma counselor provided a safe place for unfinished business to emerge.

Closure

I came to see my history with fresh perspective.

Sudden loss from the fire brought up my sudden loss of home and family at the age of thirteen. Life as I knew it disappeared overnight when my mom removed my sister and me from our home. I never had the chance to say goodbye or pack a suitcase.

My relationships with my stepfather, stepbrother, and stepsister were severed when we left. I also lost my animals. And I lost the creek in my backyard, so beautifully surrounded by the trees.

I asked myself, *If I could go back to that day, would I have done anything differently?* The question transported me to that day of keen sadness. I wished I could have hugged my stepdad and said goodbye. His drinking made him mean, but the person under his pain reliever was the stepdad I loved.

I would have walked through my yard and touched the bark on the trees I had often climbed. I would have packed my favorite things. And if I'd had more time to pack, maybe I could have processed our exit, too.

To finally process and bring closure to this traumatic event from my past, I bought a small suitcase and searched for significant items to place inside to represent what I had lost. I found stuffed animals—horses, donkeys, a goat. My mom even helped me find photos from the life we had left, including one of our once-happy family, a photo of the Mediterranean donkeys I had loved and groomed for hours, and a photo of our house with the yard in which I spent countless hours pretending and playing with my childhood best friend, Marissa.

She lived across the pasture I would run through to get to her house. To the suitcase, I added a photo of us together in matching dresses from our performance in the fourth-grade talent show. I even found a doll resembling Marissa.

Every photo and symbol in my suitcase reminds me of memories I don't want to disappear.

In cleaning the closets of my past, I found gifts. I contacted Marissa. We reminisced about old times. We apologized for the mistakes we had made in our youth. I felt the power of our friendship—a precious gift I cherish. I also reconnected with other friends from those middle school years. Conversations with my long-time friends were gifts of healing.

Looking back, I do have positive memories of that time. My mom did go back to bring us our dog and fat country cat. She sacrificed to keep my sister and me in the same school district so we could be with our friends.

I respect my mom's courage. Her decision to make a new life for us was the right one. My sister and I learned lessons that made us strong. We learned not to take what we have for granted. Those challenges from our youth turned us into women full of compassion for others.

The fire kindled conversations with my mom and sister about the difficult times in each of our lives. We talked about the day we left our home and discussed what had been too painful to address at the time. Mom filled in parts of the story I couldn't have understood as a thirteen-year-old. Because we talked, all three of us opened doors to places that needed restoration—another gift.

Like viewing movies from my past, now I could see the orchestrated details of divine provision during a time when I needed support. Middle school is a turbulent time for teens, even without the additional chaos I experienced. And thankfully, my homeroom teachers befriended me. They spent time with me outside of class. Plus, I met Kristin, a classmate who became my best friend. We were inseparable through middle school and high school. She loved animals as much as I did and lived out in the country. We rode her horses and enjoyed countless hours together. Being included with Kristin and her family filled a need I didn't even know I had.

Divine intervention replaced my losses with friendships. God knew me before I knew Him—nothing else adequately explains the far-sighted provisions made for me in my childhood.

Another gift on my healing journey was the restoration of my relationship with my dad. His drinking had wrecked our family. But a few years before the fire, he got sober—after nearly drinking himself to death. He and his wife had been living on vodka for months, which ended only after an ambulance took her to the morgue and my dad to the hospital.

After his release from the hospital, my sister and I relocated him to an assisted living facility near her Sacramento home. His health had deteriorated so much he couldn't walk and had heart problems. We managed his affairs and visited him, expecting he'd need continued care. But he surprised us and recovered.

After nine months of physical therapy and following doctor's instructions, he returned to his home in the mountains—sober and without the wheelchair. The changes continued. Dad found faith in Jesus and that Christian faith helped him to become the dad I had always wanted.

As the child of an alcoholic, I was used to broken promises and chaos. In truth, I expected my dad to revert to his old ways. But after a decade of building trust, I knew the changes in my dad were for real. Disappointments were replaced with a new relationship. (Little girls don't outgrow their need for their dad, no matter how old they are.) In a discussion with Dad about our past relationship and our current one, my dad said, "I'm a new person. I was lost for a while, but I found my way." My little girl broken heart found her dad when he found his way. Dad's new sobriety and faith gave us new memories to replace bad ones.

Even though I had forgiven my dad years earlier, my trauma counselor said I still needed to confront past hurts with my dad in order to heal completely. My dad agreed to counseling—he needed to heal also—and joined our sessions by phone. Our desire to reconcile outweighed our discomfort in confronting skeletons of the past.

We talked. We cried. We prayed. We healed.

Not many people have the opportunity for complete reconciliation. But we did—all because of a fire.

Memorials Make it Easier to Say Goodbye

The work I did to process old memories refreshed my spirit. My positive memories provided mental images to hold onto. Goodbyes are easier when we have memorials, like the suitcase I filled. A bench to sit on, a necklace to wear, a tree to sit under—they connect us to the invisible. Memorials provide a place to remember, something to touch to fill the void of our loss.

Our trees at the yellow house reminded me of my childhood home in the country. Beautiful, mature trees had surrounded that house like an atrium of security and had provided a refuge when I needed a place to think. I relived that loss when our trees burned in the fire.

After our lot was cleared, I had several opportunities to remove the dead trees, but couldn't bear losing them. Their charred skeletons were my last visual connection to what I had lost.

Journal Entry

October 2012
(four months after the fire)

The Trees, My Friends, My Loss

The breeze touches me through the music
　of rustling leaves
Leaves dance in the breeze to woo me
A whisper of goodness dances through
　sparkles of light
Strength of the branches and trunk shelter me
Their faithful presence assures me

Awesome is looking up into the sky
　through the leaves glistening with light
My friends because they always remain,
　especially through a storm

I am a tree
My strength covers and protects others
I change when seasons change
In this season, I grieve
I feel the storm stretch me
The wind tears off my dead leaves and branches
I shed my loss

Memorial of Hope

The day the tree trimming company cut down my burned-out trees, I felt like my insides had been shredded.

To fill the void, I found an artist to carve the stump of my largest pine into a memorial of hope. I wanted the memorial to symbolize the same nurturing and care our neighbors showed one another when we rebuilt our neighborhood.

The artist positioned the mama bear facing the street and the baby bear, peeking over her shoulder, facing the windows of our house. The memorial stands behind our house near a busy road and a walking path. I wanted people who passed by to enjoy the memorial.

The day the bears were fully formed, I watched people walk by and admire them. People in cars held up traffic to take photos. A lady walking by stopped to look at the bears, and I will never forget the look of pleasure reflected on her face. The bears stand to this day as a symbol of a community of neighbors who nurtured each other while they grieved and rebuilt.

With the carving complete, the bears empowered me to

testify about care and restoration. I replaced devastation with a memorial that made people smile.

We created beauty out of a stump of pain.

Celebrate Small Victories

Waves of grief exhausted me after the fire. Cruelly, the weight of my grief had even frozen my creativity and spontaneity.

My husband took over in the kitchen. When he worked out of town, we ate frozen or fast food. But nine months after the fire, I found myself in my kitchen. With all the cupboards open, three pots on the stove, and chocolate chip cookies in the oven, I paused. I felt normal—something I hadn't felt in a long time. I celebrated the moment.

I also celebrated the day when my adventurous spirit revived. I'm the person who takes the jumps on ski runs and leaps the boulders in a raging creek. This part of me had shut down after my crisis. But one year after the fire, our family went to Florida for a vacation. Never having surfed, I took lessons with my teens. How crazy is that? This middle-aged mama rode a surfboard.

I felt the weights of grief fall off me. Moments like these were worthy of celebration.

Heartache purged layers of baggage I didn't know I carried.

Gifts hide under the layers of grief. Thankfully, I found mine.

As I rebuilt the foundation of my heart, the time came to rebuild my house.

Chapter 17

How We Turned Our Trouble Into Treasure

A SMOOTH LOT with fresh dirt erased the evidence of destruction. All of the rubble had disappeared, as if nothing had ever happened. And with the excavation completed, a blank canvas invited a new beginning.

I returned to the site, expecting to feel sad. Instead, new growth welcomed me. Blades of emerald grass were popping up out of the earth, fertilized by the fire. The only piece of my house that remained was my driveway, so I stood on it and sighed, relieved to feel hopeful.

A family of deer gathered nearby to nibble the grass. I took photos to remind me of this special day.

I wanted our house back as quickly as possible. Putting my life back together meant focusing on the rebuild. Over the next few weeks, rapid progress encouraged me. After clearing the lot, they built wooden forms for the footers. Those footers would lay under the foundation and support the weight of the house. After the forms were set and the reinforcing steel secured, concrete would be poured.

I drove by after work and parked in my driveway. The forms filled with new concrete surprised me—I didn't realize this was the day the workers were to complete the footers.

I flung open the car door and rushed down the hill. The smooth surface of the concrete foundation there invited me to carve words of hope in it that would support our new home.

I dug my fingernail into the fresh concrete. Immediately, I knew the words I wanted to write:

Beauty for ashes. Joy for mourning.

My Bible was at home, so I called my husband to look up more verses for me. Then I hunted down a burned nail from another lot and carved the words found in Joshua 24:15 (KJV):

As for me and my house, we will serve the Lord.

Rex wanted me to carve Deuteronomy 3:24 (New Living Translation), which he read to me:

> *O Sovereign LORD, you have only begun to show your greatness and the strength of your hand to me, your servant. Is there any god in heaven or on earth who can perform such great and mighty deeds as you do?*

But the verse was too long and my hands ached from carving the semi-hard cement, so I carved the Bible book, chapter, and verse. The last verse I carved was:

> *Hear, O Israel: The LORD our God, the LORD is one.*
> Deuteronomy 6:4 (NIV)

I chose this verse because I knew this Jewish prayer, referred to as the Shema, would be dear to Bill, my Jewish tenant.

Words of faith would hold the weight of my house and support the people who live there.

I smiled.

Foundation Day

The footers hardened while construction workers built the foundation forms. Cement would be poured the next day. The person in charge told me I would want to watch the concrete team pour the foundation. His eyes lit up when he told me about the massive production, machinery, and workers. He suggested I take my kids out of school to watch.

The next day, Rex and I picked up Andrea and Caleb from school and headed over to the lot. I felt silly taking my kids out of school to watch cement trucks. But when we arrived, my mouth dropped in awe.

There were so many trucks and machines filling our cul-de-sac we had to park down the street. The deafening clatter and beeping sounded like enough activity to build a city block. I took in the sounds of life as they raised our house from the dead. I smiled and waved when I caught the eye of the man I had met the day before. He smiled back at me with a look that said, *I knew you wouldn't want to miss this.*

We cut through a neighbor's property to get to the hill behind our lot to watch. Two cement trucks, one with a massive mechanical arm, towered over the forms to pour cement into the molds. One worker guided the three-story-high arm as he balanced on the eight-inch ledges of the foundation walls. Other workers packed and smoothed the wet cement. A dozen people worked in unison. For them, this was a normal day of work. For us, the day signified new life.

Later that evening, the kids and I came back to carve more words of hope into the foundation. We carved our names and the names of our tenants who were living in the house when it burned.

This was a day to remember.

Writing on the Walls

After the foundation solidified, the rebuild went fast. Within a month, the frame was up. The house became real. I wanted to write on the drywall before the workers textured the walls. Our family invited friends to have a wall-writing party. We decorated the walls with pictures, words of hope, and blessings. Knowing words from the hearts of my friends live in the walls of our house reminds me of the power of optimism.

Susan: Pillar of Strength

Susan found strength in her four grandsons and teenage daughter. She defied tragedy and became the pillar her family needed to move forward and heal. In an interview with Fox 31 Denver after the fire, Susan said, "I can't walk around feeling sorry for myself. There are people to consider. If I fall apart, what's going to happen? We are all together. We're safe and it's just stuff we lost. We can replace it. We will always have the memories."

Susan's insurance company provided a rental house for her family. Friends offered to help Susan with her children so she could take care of necessary business. People gave her family items they needed.

"Everyone I knew, as well as strangers, reached out to help us. Their kindness and generosity sustained us."

Kristin: Teamwork

Kristin's husband is an architect who knows building code and the best construction materials. His knowledge made their decision to rebuild much easier. The hundreds of decisions that have to be made about everything from house plans to finishing details can overwhelm anyone—decisions can be even more difficult for someone traumatized by loss. Doug made decisions easy for Kristin by limiting her choices.

"For each decision, such as picking hardware or paint, Doug gave me about three choices. That way, I made decisions about the house, but they didn't overwhelm me."

Doug also used his expertise to advise other families as they rebuilt their houses. His support empowered them—especially at a time when so many people felt helpless.

"Helping others and having a supportive husband made dealing with the aftermath of the fire easier."

Kristin chuckled when she recalled the day her family moved into their new home. "With about twelve helpers to unload our U-Haul, unloading took about twelve minutes. Our helpers asked if there was more and we said, 'Nope. There isn't much to move when you lose everything.'

"We had lots of helpers along the way, too. Everybody helped each other, and together we made it through the process of recovery."

Thomas: Core Values Honored

Thomas found hope in the simple truths that make our country great.

After the firefighters contained the fire in Mountain Shadows, he and his neighbors watched a fire fighter, a police officer, and a couple of neighbors raise the American flag on the mountain at the top of his street. This act reminded Thomas, a veteran Marine, of the historic photo of the flag raised by Marines on Iwo Jima in 1945. When the flag was lifted, so was his spirit.

"Seeing the flag symbolized that the area was secure. Together, we would restore our community. Disasters bring out the best in Americans and show her true colors—sacrifice, service, and honor.

"Our community became more connected than before the fire. My neighbors rebuilt their houses. Human resiliency reassured me."

Photo by Anne Kraetzer

Deb: From Chaos to Calm

Deb, Denny, and her daughter's family moved into temporary housing after the Black Forest fire. After about a month, the two families moved into Deb and Denny's rental property, where they had lived years earlier.

The house was a wreck when the tenants moved out and Deb couldn't rest until she had a place that felt like home, so they took on the renovation using insurance money. The house was noisy and chaotic with the pounding, tiling, and painting; the constant flow of furniture deliveries; chatter about decisions to make; and dogs barking.

After two months of renovating and decision-making, the families were settled. Her daughter's family moved to the main floor while Deb and Denny moved into the downstairs apartment.

"We are content with our small living space and having our grandchildren live with us. We have what is important to us."

Part of reclaiming Deb's life was letting go of the belongings she lost. She found a creative way to grieve. "I prayed, 'God, show me everything I lost, one at a time. Help me forget each item so I never remember that I had it.' Thinking of an item allows me to grieve each loss and let it go. When I enter an antique store, sometimes it's hard. The furniture reminds me of the antiques and family heirlooms I lost. The process of acknowledging the items I lost and releasing them heals me.

"I used to have five teapots. I found one in an antique store and bought it. That one represents all of those from my past. I no longer felt the need to have four more. When I'm with someone, I'll say, 'I had one of these,' and I'll put it down. If I have already replaced an item in my mind, like the teapot, I no longer have any desire for it. It's really strange."

Ann's Story

Ann was twelve years ahead of us in her healing process, because her home in Los Alamos had burned in 2000. Her wisdom was a lifeline that pulled me into a hopeful place.

"You will put your life back together and feel whole again," she told our support group. "It took me about five years to start to feel like myself."

Ann's words soothed the part of me that was tangled up in insurance paperwork and overwhelming emotion. She read her thoughts to our support group, written three months after the fire that destroyed her town and home.

Ann Greene: Some Thoughts After Cerro Grande

At 2:18 p.m. on Thursday, May 11, the Cerro Grande wildfire devoured our house.

I accepted the fact that our house was gone. At first, the memories of what each room looked like and felt like were incredibly clear. My memory scrolled through my past as if I had a virtual reality access to the entire house, but only visually—no touching allowed.

How I wish I could have had a few minutes in the house to remove a few special things: Steve's medicine bear, the small wooden chest my great-grandfather brought from Germany in 1847 with all his earthly belongings inside, a favorite sweater, some of the paintings collected over the years. Given a chance to go back, I wouldn't need much time or a lot of space for the things I really miss.

The fire streamlined our life-ship and converted excess baggage to cash. It's a freeing experience. Our options are far more open than they would have been without the fire.

Our life-ship may be streamlined, but we lost our harbor. The emotional realm we are exploring is vastly unpredictable. One day or hour is bright—sunny and calm. All is well. Then the next day or hour brings a violent storm, tossing us unexpectedly toward the rocks. Next comes a heavy fog. It is impossible to see a foot ahead. How can we navigate through this?

We can't do it alone. I've learned no man or woman is an island.

Without my husband, Steve, this would have been unbearable. Our families, friends, faith community, and co-workers gave us a sense of security when we needed support. I loved the community of Los Alamos from the day I first visited in 1982. I didn't realize how much it could love me back.

The state of New Mexico has become a community because of Cerro Grande. I think we have all come to realize how vulnerable we are to the power of nature and how much we need each other to survive.

Each of us found our own way to process our loss. I found strength in carving words of faith into the foundation and walls of my new house. Susan found strength in her children and grandchildren. Kristin and her family found strength in their neighborhood community—serving others in need benefited their own recovery. Thomas found encouragement in people who cared. Carolyn became her own safe haven through her willingness to grow from her experience. She became a safe haven for others by building a support group. Deb and Denny's faith grew stronger. Ann and her husband clung to each other and their community. Donna and Rick's relationship grew stronger. The loss of their grandchildren to the fire solidified their faith in God and trust in each other.

All of us found strength.

We defied adversity with resilience.

The common thread was relationship—with others, our faith, and ourselves.

Section Four

Gifts From the Ashes

Chapter 18

How to Support Me

CRISIS DRAWS OUT our vulnerability—we need people.

A kind touch or a phone call from someone who knows us or from strangers who offer their resources refreshes our spirits just when we really need it.

After my house burned, I did a rotten job of communicating to friends and coworkers about my loss. I didn't know what to tell them. Friends wanted to show support, but they may not have known how. I found that I would rather people say the wrong words to me than to say nothing at all.

For me, a wall of silence was worse than abrasive words spoken with a motive of kindness. And when people did attempt to express support, I learned to receive their kindness, even if their words hurt.

Empathize With Me

Many times people said to us, "It's just *stuff*. You can replace the things you lost."

We said the same words ourselves, "It's just *stuff*. It's just *stuff*." The words appealed to the logical part of our brains. Things can be replaced—people can't. True. We were grateful for our safety, but many of us felt a hole in our beings, as if part of us had been ripped away. And many of us didn't understand those feelings. We were not sad about losing our stuff because we were materialistic. Our stuff is dear to us because our belongings are connections to memories we can't buy, replace, or recapture.

I came to understand that the present dissolves without our permission and fades into the past with each passing minute. Our experiences turn to memories that contribute to the person we are—our essence.

No matter how hard we try to remember faces and places, memories blur with time. Mementos, photos, handwritten letters, souvenirs, and traditions connect us to our loved ones, especially those who have passed. My friend's mother died when Ellen was twenty-two. "As time passed, I couldn't remember my mother's face," Ellen said. "I felt fear and shame at forgetting the face of such an important person as my mother. When her image blurred, that was the worst part of the grief, almost to the level of being unbearable."

Our memories fail us. Why do we forget the things we want to remember and remember the things we wish to forget? In the fire, people lost tangible memories of their loved ones. Then our sadness from the loss of our belongings grieves us. Because when connections sever, our essence fractures.

Your Presence Comforts Me

When a friend goes through a rough time, my nature is to try to make them feel better. But I must resist the urge to talk too much. Sometimes pain needs a quiet presence, not words.

It's easier to try to disperse pain by offering solutions.

Silence makes pain weigh more. People need time to honor their loss by feeling the burden. When I'm quiet, my friend's pain floats over to me. Like humidity, the weight of their pain sticks. I want to be the friend who is willing to sit and absorb the weight of their pain.

As one mental health professional said, "Do more listening with your hearts than with your ears. Listen more and talk less."

A valuable friend listens. Good listeners pay attention. They know when to wait and sense the right time to speak.

Journal Entry

September 2012
(three months after the fire)

Memories Burned Fracture Our Essence

(written from the perspective as if I had lost everything)

On my way down the path, I passed a well-meaning person who asked how I was doing.

"I'm doing all right," I said.

"At least you have your memories. Nothing can take those from you."

"Yes." I smiled and walked ahead.

I restrain myself from reacting to my bubbling anger. What? Do you know my house burned down? Do you know I lost my child's kindergarten handprints carefully molded on the plate that hung on the wall? And do you know I lost the painting that hung on the wall in my grandmother's house most of her life? My visual link to my deceased Gram was burned!

After the fire, I accidentally drive to my burnt house instead of my temporary residence. I feel so stupid.

I reach to open a can and then remember I have no can opener.

I can't sleep. Again, I can't sleep.

Will I ever sleep?

Once I sleep, I have nightmares. The worst one is of the mama cat that had seven kittens—one at a time—all of them dead.

In the same nightmare, a young woman is pregnant without a partner and alone. The baby crowns. I'm the only person available to help? *Me? Oh no!* I'm inadequate for this task, but I comfort the distressed woman. I hold my hands in position to receive life. The baby emerges dead—with a crushed skull. I hold the broken baby. Speechless—I wake up.

Is there any peace?

Ask Me Questions About My Experience

I carried a colossal bag of sad. Only a few people know what I went through to unload my grief. But instead of wasting energy being angry at people for not understanding, I made it a habit to say something like, "Even though we didn't live in our house when it burned, my loss affected me the same as if I had lost everything."

People want to be supportive and they may not know how. Sometimes we need to help them. By giving information about my experience, I honored my own feelings and, at the same time, opened a door to a more in-depth conversation.

When people asked me questions, thinking about the answers helped me process my experience.

Allow Me to Interpret My Story

Loved ones long to make us feel better, but sometimes they make judgments unintentionally.

Deb said, "It's better to let me do the talking. *I* can say, 'It was only stuff I lost,' but it's not okay for *you* to say to me, 'It was only stuff.' *I* can say, 'I am better off after losing everything,' but it's not okay for *you* to make the same statement. Allow me to be the one to make judgment statements about my story and my feelings. I need to decide the facts about what I've been through. I don't want anyone else to interpret my story unless I grant them permission."

After catastrophic loss, the two things we have left are our stories and our feelings. When someone speaks for us, we lose our voice, too.

Don't Use Your Own Experience as a Reference Point

No one can understand what another person has gone through without living the same experience.

My natural response to people in pain is to empathize using

my experiences as a reference point, but I have learned not to interpret the details of another person's story. I can't presume to know what someone has been through based on my own experience.

People assumed I should be fine because the home I lived in didn't burn. With a sigh of relief they said, "Oh…you lost a *rental* house," as if my loss should not have hurt me. They decided *for* me how I should feel. In their opinion, I wasn't one of the people who had suffered a real loss.

Allow Me to Feel Without Fixing Me

Six weeks after the fire, a friend of mine was sifting through the ashes of his burned home. In the ashes, he found the bones of his family's two cats. He knew they had always counted on him to take care of them. But he hadn't been able to protect them when they needed him the most.

In the weight of his grief, he didn't want to be fixed. He needed to be allowed to feel whatever feelings came up without criticism or judgment. A supportive friend understands that expressing emotions helps you process your pain, even if your feelings don't make sense to them at the moment.

Creative Ways to Help

"Don't ask, 'What do you need?' Be a snoop and find out what I need. Just do it. That's what friends do," Donna and Rick said. "Give me a hug and say, 'I'm here for you.'"

Pay attention. Ask questions. Observe. Think about what you would need if you were in the same situation. If you don't have time, send money for a special dinner out. If a friend in need has children, they probably need help transporting or watching them.

Kristin said, "Having three kids, I needed people to watch my children so I could set up a new home for our family.

I needed life to be normal as soon as possible for my kids. We needed normalcy, which couldn't happen until we established the necessary structure. I needed time to shop and settle a temporary home."

See Me Through My Crisis
Over an Extended Period of Time

Most people show compassion in the early weeks after a traumatic event, but soon they "forget" and their support fades. Grief, however, is a process that takes longer than we would like—weeks, months, years—so don't make the mistake of assuming I am okay.

"Most people in our lives have a limited capacity to support a long-term need," Deb said. "Friends and acquaintances showed up to help my family sift our ashes and clear the dead trees off our land. But a few months after our crisis, support tapered off. Most people didn't want to talk about our loss anymore. They stopped asking us questions. There is an undefined period of time during which people will tolerate listening to the same problem.

"After the Waldo Canyon fire, many people wanted us to stop thinking about our grief. The unaffected moved on in their own lives, even though we were in the thick of putting our lives back together."

Continue to reach out after time passes.

Ask me how I am doing. I may say I'm fine, but I'm probably not. I'd rather you ask too many questions than ignore me because you don't know what to say. Trust me to let you know if I don't want to talk. I enjoy spending time with people who ask probing questions to make me think. When you ask me details about what I'm going through, I feel valued, especially when I feel your sincerity.

> Your courage, strength, and faith during these challenging times stands as inspiration for us all. Thank you for being, open to the possibility of love and true wisdom.
>
> May your paths be illuminated by all that is good and prosperous.

Don't Underestimate the Power of Words Spoken From the Heart

Heart-felt empathy comforted me more than anything. Colorado College held an exhibit of poetry and photos from victims of the Waldo Canyon fire. Their expressions of grief evoked deep empathy from visitors. Many pinned handwritten notes to the wall in response to the brokenhearted. I choked up when I read the kind words of compassion expressed by strangers.

I Couldn't Express My Gratitude at the Time

Gestures of kindness soak into the places that need healing. In the aftermath of the Colorado fires, lovely people like the Samaritan's Purse crews showed up to serve. Volunteers, organizations, churches, and businesses offered their time, talent, and resources.

The American Red Cross provided displaced families shelters, personal necessities, and counseling. In the first two days of the Waldo Canyon evacuation, the Salvation Army mobile kitchens provided more than 2,000 meals. Care and Share provided food for months. Donors provided cash gifts and food. Businesses provided goods and discounts. Generosity from the community inspired our Colorado Springs region.

The deluge of stress after the crisis prevented most of us from doing something we wanted to do—express the gratitude we felt but didn't have the energy to give. I didn't write proper "thank you" notes to people who deserved them.

Too much time passed to write notes that should have been written long ago. I still feel guilty. These are the words I want to say to the people who didn't receive a thank you letter:

Dear Givers in my time of distress,
I will never forget kind words spoken, the businesses that provided discounts and gifts, the faces of volunteers who offered their time.

And I will never forget my colleagues who helped me pull myself together and make it through the day, the strangers who didn't know my name, but served because they cared.

Your acts of kindness didn't go unnoticed. Your spirit of love soaked into the dark places in our hearts. You invested in us and we will pass on your goodness in the future. We may be in a crowd serving you or your children someday.

Relationships Change After a Crisis

After trauma, people change—sometimes for a season and sometimes permanently. I wasn't myself after the trauma I had experienced. People wanted to talk about normal things. But nothing was normal for me.

A colleague would ask, "How are you?" But that simple question sent me into a tailspin. I scrolled through intense emotions and tried to find an answer.

"Good," I would say. An honest answer would have required a two-hour sit-down conversation.

I found being alone much easier than engaging in trivial talk. Crowds overwhelmed me. I declined invitations to social events for a time until I felt I could stand on solid ground. I appreciated the invitations, but needed to save my energy. Most of the time, I didn't attend much of anything.

I had to keep processing my grief in ways that didn't make sense to people who knew me. To some, my persistent thoughts appeared irrational and my fears illogical. But my faithful friends trusted me to come out on the other side of the crisis and waited patiently for me to recover.

The presence of a friend during a dark time soothes brokenness. We remember the people who care about us. We remember the people who show up in our darkest hours. And sometimes, special people appear in our lives when we least expect it.

Maryann was one of those people.

Chapter 19

The Friend Who Became a Gift

MARYANN'S STORY was the most difficult to write, even more difficult than my own.

Her pain clung to the pits of my own unresolved pain. Both of us were misfits in the aftermath of the Waldo Canyon fire. My house had burned, but not the house I lived in. Her house hadn't burn, but it might have been easier if it had. We understood each other.

I found Maryann two years after the fire. Her name was in an old newspaper article written just after the fire. I'm not an intrusive person, but I wanted to interview someone whose home had survived. I left a message on her home phone, but didn't expect her to return my call.

A few days later, she left a message on my answering machine. Surprised, I called her back and explained my book project. I tried to put her at ease by letting her know I wasn't a journalist with an angle for a story—nothing would be printed without her permission.

A week later, we met for lunch. We were still consumed in conversation when the servers filled the last salt and pepper shakers. Prompted by the sound of the vacuum in the empty restaurant, we chatted all the way out the door and into the parking lot. When I left the restaurant, I knew I had met a special friend.

Ironically, Maryann met with me on that day to say she didn't want to be part of my book. But her mother's maxim kept ringing in her ears, *Do not judge others before you give them a chance*. She met with me face-to-face just to be polite.

After we met, she decided to risk sharing her story with me. Over two years after the Waldo Canyon fire, Maryann hadn't recovered from the trauma. Her pain was still raw, like it had happened yesterday.

The newspaper article that led me to Maryann had caused her great pain and created a terrible misunderstanding between Maryann and her neighbors. Shortly after the fire, the local newspaper interviewed her because her house had survived. But they edited her story in a way that made her sound cold-hearted and jealous of her neighbors (because they would have new homes in the end). The opposite was true.

"Knowing the article altered my neighbors' perceptions of me hurt," Maryann said. "My heart broke for them. The editor had twisted my words to sound like I didn't care." With tears in her eyes she said, "I can't even imagine what my neighbors went through."

Through her living room window, day after day, she watched her neighbors drive to the ruins of their homes. They got out of their cars and stared. She felt tremendous guilt knowing her house had survived and theirs had burned.

Desperate to ease the pain of her neighbors, each day she opened her garage. She filled an ice chest full of water and food. She set up chairs to offer a refuge from the heat and mess. Aside from the few neighbors who stopped by, the chairs remained empty and the ice chest full. Compassion through provision overflowed from her home like a thoughtful gift wrapped in love. But it was left—intentionally unopened.

The emptiness of her garage and rejection of her offers to help built a chasm between her and her neighbors. Not because they'd done anything wrong. Not because she herself had done anything wrong. Rather, grief separated them like an impenetrable fog.

"Looking back, I should have been more forceful in helping. I should have showed up and started sifting with them. At the time, I wanted to respect their personal space, otherwise I would've felt like an intruder going through their bedroom and personal drawers. I regret not being more persistent in helping sort through their ashes.

"In my attempt to be respectful, I didn't do enough."

A hand held out but not taken felt like the worst kind of isolation. Combined with her misconstrued words from the newspaper article, Maryann was misunderstood and alone in her experience. Support from the community was plentiful for those with a total loss, but not for people in her situation. After perceived rejection, she withdrew and became depressed.

Feeling overwhelmed, she needed to repair the heat and smoke damage in her own home. But when she and her husband initiated the insurance claim process, it became a nightmare. A year before the fire, they had spent thousands of dollars to replace all the windows in their house. Now, the heat from the fire had sucked the glass from the frames, making them unusable. The fire voided the warranty that came with the new windows.

Maryann walked the home owner's insurance claim representative through her house. She showed him the damaged cabinets and woodwork, all brittle because of the ruined wood glue.

The rep said, "It's not covered."

She showed him where the wallpaper edges were curled from the heat and where it had melted so tightly to the wall that the texture showed through.

"It's not covered."

She pointed out how the hardwood floors creaked because the heat had distorted the structural integrity.

"This is all from natural wear and tear," he said.

She showed him the front door that looked sun damaged, even though no sunlight hit the enclosed porch.

"This is not caused by the fire."

Maryann pointed out the nails that had popped out of the exterior siding.

"It's not covered."

"We just bought this patio table. We know how much we paid for it. The firefighters broke it with their hoses as they tried to save our house."

"It's not covered."

And Maryann told me, "The insurance company wanted to give us piddle for the table along with everything else."

All in all, the insurance representative treated Maryann like she was overreacting and trying to get more than she deserved. Speaking up took all her strength because she already felt guilty asking for anything, knowing her neighbors had lost everything.

The battle exhausted Maryann and her husband. Then, "Professionals carrying briefcases came around the neighborhood. Men handed out business cards advertising they could help us with our claims. My husband looked them up online. The website looked legitimate. The representatives said they worked with the insurance companies. They knew the legal guidelines and insurance process, so they could ensure fair practice. The representatives convinced us they could help us at a time when we desperately needed support. With everything else we had on our plate, we didn't have time to research everything. We signed a contract on an iPad. We figured the ten percent they would keep would be worth the help on our claim."

Sadly, the "public adjusters" turned out to be crooks who had flown in from Georgia, a company that preyed on disaster victims. Maryann and her husband didn't know that, once they hired a public adjuster, their insurance company would consider them a third party and refuse to talk to them about their own claim. The scam company gave Maryann the runaround, refusing to give her the paperwork she needed to stay informed.

"Our insurance company sent the public adjusters the money from our claim," she said. "We didn't see a check until after they took their cut. We never got any paperwork showing us the allocation for the damage or what the insurance company paid. The ordeal was one big mess."

In the end, the crooks took thirty percent of Maryann's claim money. The remaining money barely touched the cost of repairs to their home.

In addition to the damage to their home, they also lost business merchandise. "Six years before the fire, we closed our floral gift shop. We stacked all the stock from our store in one stall of our garage," she said. "The heat ruined everything. We had a separate business policy on our business items, but we got pennies compared to what we lost."

Four years after the fire, most problems with their house were not resolved. They had had to use a sizable amount of savings for repairs on their house.

The first time I met Maryann, I shared pieces of my story with her. We must have been talking about survivor's guilt when I shared my story about the quilt. Colorado Springs Together, the community center assembled for fire victims, distributed resources from the community. Businesses, churches, and individuals gave free items. Businesses offered generous discounts. Hundreds affected by the Waldo Canyon fire felt an abundance of goodwill. Since I hadn't lost my personal items in the fire, I didn't participate in receiving the gifts offered. In my women's support group, I heard about quilts that teams of people made for those who had lost their homes. The thought of having a quilt to wrap around my grief, made by people who cared, appealed to me. The quilt was the one item I would ask for.

I didn't feel worthy of the gift in light of the others who had lost much more than me, but I mustered up my courage and pulled open the doors to Colorado Springs Together. The lady sitting at the table by the entrance caught my eye. I used the table to hold myself up, wishing I hadn't come. It wasn't easy to ask a stranger to give me a gift. It would have been much easier to be on the other side of the table.

I introduced myself. The words jumped out of my mouth, "I understand you have quilts for the people who lost their homes."

The lady behind the desk said, "Yes, what is your address?"

"2557 Hot Springs Court."

She flipped through the pages of addresses. She placed her finger on mine. She said, "Someone already picked up a quilt for your address."

"That must have been Bill and Elaine, my tenants. I am the owner of the house."

She looked at me as if I was trying to cheat the system. "Your address is already checked off. I can't give you a quilt."

I swallowed my embarrassment and walked to my car, crushed. *I didn't deserve the quilt anyway.* Survivor's guilt throbbed like a second heartbeat. I sat in my car and absorbed the jab.

I remember the look on Maryann's face when I told her the story. Her face mirrored the pain I felt. To cover it, I transitioned into my *I'm tough* mode.

Maryann and I continued to stay in contact. About a year later, we set a time to meet before Christmas. I knew she had lost many of her Christmas ornaments to heat damage. I found an adorable rabbit enclosed in glass, which symbolized hope to me after the fire. I wrote her a note explaining how a rabbit sat in the rubble the day I first saw the ruins of my house. I printed out the story from my journal, "Rabbits Talk."

Maryann handed me a gift bag. I pulled out a small pine tree ornament with a note from the artist Vinny Luciani which read, "Colorado has experienced great personal and public loss due to recent wildfires...these ornaments are hand-crafted from trees burned in those fires. They represent the theme of beauty, rebirth and hope that can come out of devastating destruction."

With teary eyes I squeezed the tree in my hand, feeling the power in the gift. But that wasn't all. Maryann told me she had another gift for me. She told me she made it with love and I would have to view it that way because it wasn't perfect. She walked me into her living room and we dragged a large gift bag back into the kitchen.

I rustled the tissue paper and lifted heavy fabric from the bag. Shocked, I felt a flood of warmth fill me. Tears welled. I knew she had made me a quilt. I pulled it out and held it to my chest.

"You made me a quilt. I can't believe you made me a quilt." The best kind of tears cleansed all wounds and healed my heart in that moment. Both of us sobbed.

With my heart full, I unfolded the quilt. On each color-ful fold, I admired sapphire blue and purple set against black. Then something yellow caught my eye. I stood and shook open the rest of the folds. Set in the center of the quilt—was my yellow house. Crafted with perfection, the image of my two-story house with white trim and a grey roof erased a multitude of losses.

Maryann had never made a quilt before. For me, she pulled out her dusty sewing machine and bought the special attach-ments needed for the details on my quilt. A little old lady shopping in the fabric store gave her tips and encouragement.

She worked for months to express her heart through stitches filled with love. And she did it not only for me, but also for the others who had lost their homes and for whom she didn't have an outlet to express her compassion.

The closer I looked the more detail I noticed. Maryann had stitched a red heart on the front door and a little dog in front of the house. She made trees and bushes like the ones that used to surround my house. I wrapped the quilt around me, deeply feeling all of Maryann's love.

Maryann asked if my house was yellow. Shocked, I said, "You haven't seen a photo of my house?" I thought she had because the house in the center of the quilt looked exactly like mine.

"No. I thought you said it was yellow, but I wasn't sure."

"You have to see my house. It looks like the one on the quilt." We hopped into my car and drove the two miles to my rebuilt yellow house.

Maryann stared at the house, then we took photos of me holding the quilt in front of the house.

What are the chances of Maryann handcrafting a house out of fabric that looked exactly like the one I lost?

I felt invisible hands from above touch me with a perfect gift and a special friendship. Isn't that how God works? Good out of bad, relationships out of isolation. My belief proved true: All things work together for good.

The newspaper article that had caused Maryann so much pain was the same article that eventually brought us together at a time when Maryann had been alone, misunderstood, and wounded.

She told me, "The fire brought us together to be each other's angels."

I agreed. Throughout the disaster, friendship wove us together in a tapestry of love, the strong kind of love that overcomes and helps people thrive.

Chapter 20

Hope After Devastation

LIFE IS SIMPLER NOW. Only a few things are deeply important to me.

Now, our important papers are in a box and ready to go should we ever need to evacuate again. I sent my photos and videos to cyber sites so they can't burn. A flash drive with important documents stays in my purse.

When we evacuated our home, I clung to my precious items. But I couldn't hang on to them—they were like liquid in my hands. My efforts to protect my important things made me realize that nothing really belonged to me. Their significance was in the memories attached to them. In the end, that was enough for me.

In time, new strength grew by the power of the invisible hands that nurtured me. My faith taught me that relationships can transfigure every ugly thing on this Earth. I have witnessed the effect when people lift each other out of the pit of despair. I have watched faith renewed by small gifts from the fire, such as Bill and Elaine's menorah.

Things that used to bother me before the fire don't bother me anymore. Unexpected changes in plans used to annoy me—these days, I adjust more easily. Now, when I've arranged my day around an appointment and the person doesn't show up, I'm not fazed. When I see mounds of rubble, I know about the treasure hiding inside. When an angry person throws up his arms and curses down the grocery aisle, I wonder about the pain under their anger. If I notice a person who has an addiction, I understand the kind of desperate pain that aches for just one moment of relief.

After the rebuild of our house was complete, I hoped Bill and Elaine would move back into the house. When they declined, I wanted my family to move in. Those hopes were crushed due to circumstances beyond my control, so Rex and I decided we would continue to rent our yellow house to others and stay in our Manitou Springs home.

Since I had to "let go" of the house I had put my heart, energy, and time into, I wrote the letter below to process my feelings.

Journal Entry

April 2013

(ten months after the fire)

Dear Yellow House,

I vowed to rebuild you. I kept my promise.

After your restoration, I wanted to make you my home again. My wishes didn't turn out as I hoped. Since I can't move in, I dedicate you to be a place of refuge and peace for others. May your light shine through each window into the hearts of those who dwell inside.

Help me not be sad about having to release you. I must trust that God will use you for His good purpose—a gift for others as you have been for me.

May the labor of my love be appreciated. You are not an ordinary house. You are beauty from the ashes.

Moving On

My plans didn't work out, but isn't that how life goes? Plans failed, but change made me grow. Heartaches came without my permission, but I am stronger. My effort proved I can rebuild not just a house, but relationships. The thought of the yellow house with a new family safe inside made me smile. Just a month after it was finished, a young couple with a toddler moved in. I imagine them laughing like my family did all those years ago.

Reflections

Rev. Hunting: People Are Good

"Looking back on the crisis, the world is sometimes a scary, nasty place. But at the time of the fire, I witnessed the good in people. When life is scary and ridiculous, I think back—I won't forget how our community came together. If there's a lesson to be learned by this experience it is, by and large, people are really good. When the chips are down, neighbors come together and help each other. They put aside any kind of differences to do what's right."

Susan: Let Go Or Be Dragged

"Looking back, we had three days before evacuation. I sat on my deck. I watered my plants. I packed only a few things. I remember watching my neighbor watering his yard and house. I jokingly said to him, 'Do you think watering will save your house?'

This is never going to happen. But it did. Poof! The lesson I learned was: When people give you a warning, listen. When there is a threat, it doesn't matter how ridiculous you look packing your car.

"We saved some precious items from the fire. My grandmother's sewing machine, a small hand-carved stool from my father, the hard drive from my computer, and some photos.

My grandsons took the American flag given to them when their parents died along with their parents' ashes and college diplomas. The flag and those ashes sit on my mantle, which was carved from wood that survived the fire. The soapstone bear found in the ashes sits in my living room."

In the early months after the fire, Susan brought rocks to our Wonderful Waldo Women support group. Each was carved with the words *Begin Again*. One woman had her rock laid into the concrete porch of her newly built house. Susan keeps her rock in the kitchen in her new home as a reminder. The fire forced closure on her past, but she is thankful for the blessing of the people she loves and for her future.

"My family and friends are my strength. I've learned to live and appreciate each day. Nothing can take away my memories. Everything lost was just 'stuff.' There are things that will never be replaced, such as my family heirlooms and photographs. Yet, my life is full of blessings and so much gratitude.

"We whine and complain about things in our daily life, but when we get a second chance, we must grab life with both hands and not look back. Never for one minute take for granted that tomorrow will be here. Just when you think you have it all planned out—wham!—it all changes.

"My dear friend and former neighbor, Karla, who also lost her home in the Waldo Canyon fire, passed away suddenly at age fifty-two, four years after the fire. Karla and her husband had finished rebuilding their new house not long before she passed—another reminder that every moment is a gift.

"My life motto is, *Let go or be dragged*. Four years and four months after the fire, I know we will all be okay.

We are survivors!"

Kristin: We Can Lose it All and Still Feel Whole

"The fire taught our kids lessons my husband and I couldn't have taught them in a lifetime. I learned that we can lose it all, yet still feel whole. The lessons were bitterly hard, but our journey of restoration made us better people.

"Love from strangers, neighbors, and organizations across the United States blanketed us with kindness. Others elevated our spirits and blessed us throughout our journey of healing. We want to pay it forward."

Thomas: Our Neighborhood Came Together

In his careers, Thomas has seen humanity at its worst. The Waldo Canyon fire renewed his hope in the goodness of people.

Thomas' neighbors supported each other, whether their houses burned or not.

"My neighborhood came together. We witnessed tragedy followed by togetherness and concern from our fellow man. People cared. Our community is stronger than before the fire.

"Resiliency is a big deal to me after seeing so much tragedy in my careers. Witnessing the resiliency of people in my community encouraged me."

Looking back, Thomas also reflected on the devastation of the fire and that the outcome could have been much worse. "Hundreds or thousands could have died or been injured. I am awed because the Lord saved so many people from death and injury."

Carolyn: Lessons Learned

"Devastation didn't defeat me. I survived and learned to thrive again. My life is good. I asked myself, 'What lessons am I supposed to receive from this and how can I grow from them?' I tried not to shut down when the stress overwhelmed me. I walked though my pain, open and willing to learn lessons. My willingness to stay open allowed me to heal."

Deb: Too Small to Worry About

Deb reflected two years after the Black Forest fire. She posted the following message on her Facebook account:

"Two years ago today, June 11, 2013, our lives changed in a matter of moments. When we evacuated, I carried everything I could in a great big purse. Everything else burned.

"All things work together for good. Yes, we lost all of our household goods and photographs, but amazingly our friends and family provided photos we thought we would never see again. Memories restored.

"We aren't attached to things anymore. Nothing we own has history, baby slobber, or sentimentality—sure makes life easier.

"Problems? Once you have been through something tough, other things seem too small to worry about.

"I'm grateful to those friends who put up with my funky way of healing—eyelashes on my car headlights, shopping binges, and French fries. I talked and they listened. Those who listened are true friends.

"Some people come along and say, 'I don't know how you could possibly go through losing everything and get over it.' Yes, I really got over it. I thought I wouldn't recover at the time because I lost everything. I'm in a different place now. We are adaptable human beings. We can get over adversity.

"Our life has been nothing short of amazing. We have been blessed to live inter-generationally with one of our children, our son-in-law, and five grandchildren. We have not rebuilt yet, but we've grown to be satisfied. If the day comes to re-build, we will. We have created our own cozy little space for the two of us. We couldn't be happier.

"I suspect we will eventually hold this date, June 11, as one to remember and hold dear.

A glass of wine, anyone?"

Donna and Rick: Hardship Made Us Stronger

"When you go through several traumas like we did, you can expect that your life is going to change. Our marriage is strong because we allow each other to express our feelings.

We depend on each other. Our relationship was strong before our traumas—hardship made us even stronger.

"Trauma changes relationships. We have seen other peoples' relationships end when tragedy struck their lives. We chose the path of our faith and found strength in each other. Some friends abandoned us and some friends stayed with us. You find out who your friends really are. We came out the other side of tragedy with close friends who have stuck with us through our hardships.

"We learned to trust God and go with the flow."

Ann: Gifts From the Past

During the first year after the fire, Ann received a gift from her past. Her church had an event where everyone who lost their home was given a box of Christmas ornaments. Volunteers set out tables for fire victims to pick the ornaments they wanted. There were also tables with free items to choose from. At a table in the back, Ann spotted a jigsaw puzzle she used to have. She ran her hand over the box and clutched the edges. Memories of her family gathered at her dining table putting this puzzle together warmed her. Her children had assembled that same puzzle every Christmas for over twenty years. Ann pressed the cardboard box to her chest and breathed in the stream of memories.

"I rushed to find Steve and show him what I found. The puzzle meant so much to me. Looking back, I can almost say I am glad we lost our house. Many good things came out of our loss, once the pain subsided. I have more empathy for anyone going through a natural disaster. I can support others in a way I never could have before the fire.

"We experienced compassion from people across the world. Their concern for us lifted our spirits. We felt grateful for the generosity people offered. The heightened awareness of our interdependence is a blessing to be treasured and nurtured wherever and whenever possible.

"Each of God's creatures, from the birds who greet the dawn, to the friends who listen and cry with us, to the people across the country who contribute to the Red Cross to help those in need—we are all one family. It is too bad it takes something like Cerro Grande to make us realize this."

Maryann: Small Kindnesses Made a Big Difference

"Not a day goes by when I don't think of how things could have been different. I'm so very, very sorry for everything my neighbors and other fire victims went through. I wish all of them blessings in their journey forward.

"I count among my blessings the firefighters and policemen who put their lives on the line for us. After the fire, the ravaged neighborhoods had a problem with thieves breaking into vacant houses and cars. Police officers prevented looting.

"People didn't realize the care and vigilance shown by our police officers. Officers made sure that the only people in the neighborhood were residents. They blocked off roads and checked the identification of those who entered. At nighttime, a police car blocked the entrance to our neighborhood. My husband leaves for work at 3:30 a.m. When he left each morning, floodlights hit his car from watchful policemen. We felt safe and protected. I can't express enough thanks to them.

"The community came together. Small gestures of kindness made a big difference. Strangers asked if they could give us hugs. Friends sent us gift cards to replace all the food we had to throw away. Friends invited us to stay with them when we evacuated.

"My biggest blessing is my special friend who found me from an article in the newspaper. The same article that caused me so much pain gave me the gift of a new friendship—the one good thing that came out of devastation."

My friends' responses to recovery after disaster renewed my optimism. I reflected on my own experience.

From ashes to a beautiful new house, I saw a tapestry woven from the story of my life. I found threads of beauty in my story. Ashes encourage fertile soil and new growth. I allowed the ashes in my life to change me into a stronger person and so did my friends. We can trust, bless the change, and move on to the next surprise in life.

The day I received the keys to our newly rebuilt house, I unlocked the door and stepped into the foyer. I looked ahead into the living room and through the giant picture windows. Sun shone through time into my heart. I felt the same awe I had felt years ago when I entered with the realtor and said, "Let's make an offer."

I walked by the fireplace and touched its rocks, perfect with fossils of leaves imprinted in some of the flagstone. I laid my hands on the quartz countertops in the kitchen.

After walking through every room, I sat on the stairs with my head in my hands, tears dripping my memories and the moment. I knew it was time to dance, not on the ashes but on a new beginning, my celebration of persevering.

Once again, I danced.

Journal Entry

April 2013
(nine months after the fire)

Keys

Keys come in different forms—
friendships and opportunity.

Keys turn perceived failures into unexpected
opportunities. They turn despair into
unexpected surprises.

Keys are a longing fulfilled when turned in the
door of a new home. Sometimes they open the
door to a safe place that shields us from harm.

Today, I hold the key to my new yellow house,
a key to something beautiful and full of promise.

The cool key in my hand turns the clock back to
when my house embraced me and my children.
Once our refuge, the house was reduced to a
pile of ashes.

And now, with the turn of time, it has been rebuilt.

My hands are open. I release my house,
my memories, and my past.

Epilogue

KNOWING NOW WHAT I didn't know then, if another fire threatened my home, I would get the heck out and leave. I wouldn't look back.

The first time fire threatened, I rushed to save everything. Now, I respect fire's nature—ruthless and unpredictable. The Waldo Canyon fire could have turned with erratic winds and obstructed my path.

When I wrote this book, I didn't expect to be filled with more than I had lost. The people I know now because of the fire touched me in the deepest caverns of my grief. They inspired me with their love for their families, community, and me.

I didn't set out to splatter my vulnerability on the pages of this book. After my friends shared their stories with transparency, I realized that I should be just as vulnerable. Halfway through writing *Fire of Hope*, I took the page of interview questions to my trauma counselor. I put it in her hands and asked her to interview me as I had the others. I sweated through the process of putting words to hard questions such as: What was the hardest part of the entire fire experience? How did it change you? I cried while answering the same questions I had asked others. We met more than once so I could get through my questions.

My once-tender threads of vulnerability have grown stronger. I've become stronger as a whole person. My connections with others suffering the same fate bonded us together and made us a bundle that could not be broken, instead of individuals, fragile and alone.

In our culture, at the end of the day, moms and dads click their garage door openers and disappear into their homes. Families don't know the names of their neighbors. The busyness of life exhausts us.

It took our natural disaster of flames and smoke to draw people out of their comfort zones and into relationship with their neighbors and community.

After the fire in our lives, we survived—then we thrived.

We found treasure in the rubble.

My fire story could be seen as another tragic example of life's unfairness and pain. But I know and trust that the hardships we face have redemptive purposes, as this Bible scripture assures us:

> *And we know that in all things God works for the good of those who love him, who have been called according to his purpose.* Romans 8:28 (NIV)

God has worked all things for good in Rex's and my life, too. Thirty years before we met, Rex was given a recurring dream about rescuing me from the ashes and rubble of a fire. In perfect timing, we met, married, and have been building a great life together ever since.

I have not arrived at a destination of complete healing. However, I know my recovery tools and how to use them.

I hope they help you as well.

More to Come

My journey will continue with creating a companion workbook to *Fire of Hope: Finding Treasure in the Rubble* for individual use and group study.

Contributors to
Fire of Hope

(Written five years after the fire)

Susan's family living at home at the time of the fire:
(back row) Hannah, Brandon, Susan
(front row) Justin, Conner, Tyler

SUSAN LIVES IN COLORADO SPRINGS with her daughter, Hannah, a student at UCCS, and her grandchildren: Justin, a high school senior; Tyler, a high school sophomore; Conner, a sixth-grader; her two dogs, Duffy and Jax; and Ellie, her cat. Son Logan is a twenty-nine-year-old Marine veteran, a father of three (one son and twins), and works in Colorado Springs. Her oldest grandson, Brandon, is majoring in biochemistry at the University of Maine.

From Susan's new home, eight miles away from her burned house, she can see the silhouettes of the burned trees on the hillside—a stark reminder of how life can change in a heartbeat.

"When I see the blackened trees, I remember that nobody said life would be easy. But life is certainly worth the ride. I keep my family and loved ones close and I'm stronger than I ever knew was possible."

KRISTIN AND HER FAMILY returned to Ashton Park 2.0 (same lot, house version 2) in August, 2013, with much gratitude.

Doug designed the house and kept the floor plan mostly the same, but the exterior is quite modern. They used a lot of local materials in the rebuild, including 90-year-old wood for railings and bricks from Pueblo.

"It is GREAT to be home!"

THOMAS LIVES IN MOUNTAIN SHADOWS in the same house that survived the Waldo Canyon fire. He taught criminal justice at Pikes Peak Community College and at the police academy in Colorado Springs after 20 years of service in the Los Angeles Police Department. At the time this book was written, he was working as a private detective and administering polygraphs for law enforcement.

Thomas gained appreciation for the strength and character of the people he dealt with in his community after the fire. The Colorado Springs Police Department, fire departments, and other first responders impressed Thomas with their integrity and professionalism. "I will never forget how a devastated community came together to be good neighbors to each other."

Rev. Rudy Cerullo II, Th.D, D.Min., Ph.D. has been in full-time ministry for forty-five years as a pastor, associate pastor, chaplain, missionary, and international guest speaker. He has been a professor of Biblical Studies, Theology, and Biblical Counseling for several universities. He and his wife, Lynn, now live in a different home in the same Rockrimmon area they lived in at the time of the fire.

"Had the fires consumed our possessions, we would have had what is most important—each other—and all we needed to continue to minister to others."

Son Jeff and daughter-in-law Sarah, Carolyn and son Kevin, husband Jim, daughter-in-law Gwen, granddaughter, Brooklyn and son Ryan.

Carolyn and her husband, **Jim**, built their dream retirement home away from the wildfire area that consumed their home.

They made lemonade out of lemons with gorgeous mountain views off their back patio that fill them with peace and joy! Carolyn realizes she is much more than her previous home and its contents. "Wherever I go, home is inside my soul, where the love from family and friends transcends all."

DEB AND DENNY moved from the country to a house in Colorado Springs, which they were renting out to a family at the time of the fire. They live with their daughter, son-in-law, and five grandchildren. They have not rebuilt their house, but they have rebuilt their lives. For now, they are satisfied living in a basement apartment with a hidden garden, their family, and four King Charles Cavalier Spaniels.

"We have found treasure after the rubble in our family and depth in our faith we've never known before. With each breath, we hold things loosely."

ANN AND STEVE OF LOS ALAMOS, New Mexico, now live in the home of their dreams, which they built on a lot a few miles from their former house. Moving into their new house in 2003 gave significant closure to their loss, but they still think of their lives as B.F. and A.F., Before Fire and After Fire.

"After is better! We learned that home is where we are together—so much more than just a house."

RICK AND DONNA LIVE LIFE with joy, despite their challenges. They have traveled in their RV and seen our wonderful country, the United States. They reside in an active adult community where they minister to those who need encouragement and keep busy with their children and grandchildren.

"We visit our son, Tim, in prison whenever possible and watch his faith bring others to the Lord. We have learned to trust the Lord one day at a time."

MARYANN, HER HUSBAND, DAN, and their little Yorkie named Chloe live in the same house surrounded by new construction and scarred mountains with new growth. They have four grown children, Sherry, Timothy, Justus, and Alicia. They also have eight grandchildren, one of whom they lost at birth. Maryann works from home managing her floral business and caring for two of her grandchildren after school.

"My heart will always ache for those who lost their homes and I will remain grateful for my family, home, and special friends I met because of the fire."

BILL AND ELAINE AND THEIR CATS, Shena and Otto, moved to New York City in 2013 for reasons unrelated to the fire. They now live peacefully in a spacious Queens apartment near Bill's birthplace, nearer the final resting places of his parents and grandparents, and only a half-day's drive from Elaine's living and departed

ancestors in Ithaca. Their menorah is displayed on a bookshelf in their living room. "We will always miss the views of Pikes Peak and mourn the absence of two irreplaceable relics lost in the fire, a table carved by Elaine's uncle out of a tree in her parents' backyard and Bill's grandfather's grandfather clock."

CHRISTIE LEE, MA, MFT, LPC, AAMFT is a mental health crisis care provider. She serves as a first responder for disasters with the Red Cross as a trained trauma specialist. Her expertise in trauma recovery and EMDR serves trauma victims throughout El Paso County. Her passion is for clients to heal after trauma.

"And this hope will not lead to disappointment. For we know how dearly God loves us, because he has given us the Holy Spirit to fill our hearts with his love."   *Romans 5:5 (NLT)*

End Notes

1 Stratton, Rick, Long-term Fire Analyst "The Waldo Canyon Fire: Fires on the Colorado Front Range and Home Destruction, A Report to the Pike and San Isabel National Forests." Report no. V6. July 7, 2012. Accessed March 23, 2017. http://www.wildfirelessons.net/HigherLogic/System/DownloadDocumentFile.ashx?DocumentFileKey=b7dc6d92-acd2-4685-a60f-df1fb33b6347.

2 City of Colorado Springs. "Waldo Canyon Fire 23 JUNE 2012 TO 10 JULY 2012 FINAL AFTER ACTION REPORT." Report. City of Colorado Springs. 2-110. Release Date: 3 April 2013. http://www.springsgov.com/units/communications/ColoradoSpringsFinalWaldoAAR_3April2013.pdf.

3 City of Colorado Springs. "Waldo Canyon Fire 23 JUNE 2012 TO 10 JULY 2012 FINAL AFTER ACTION REPORT." January 21, 2014. City of Colorado Springs. 2-110. https://townofmountainvillage.com/media/Black-Forest-Fire-Assessment-Team.pdf.

4 Jeffs, Victoria. "CrossRoads: A Journey of Purpose." Colorado Springs: Day2, 2014. pg 82. Print. www.FindYourDay2.com.

5 "Post Traumatic Stress Disorder (PTSD)." Mayo Clinic. © 1998-2014 Mayo Foundation for Medical Education and Research. Accessed September 25, 2014. http://www.mayoclinic.org/diseases-conditions/post-traumatic-stress-disorder/basics/definition/con-20022540.

6 Ibid.

7 Anonymous, PTSD Survivor. "What Do Body Memories Feel Like?" My PTSD Forum. March 30, 2013. Accessed October 9, 2014. https://www.myptsd.com/c/threads/what-do-body-memories-feel-like.25545/.

8 Anonymous, PTSD Survivor. "What Do Body Memories Feel Like?" My PTSD Forum. February 12, 2013. Accessed October 9, 2014. https://www.myptsd.com/c/threads/what-do-body-memories-feel-like.25545/.

9 "What is EMDR?" EMDR Institute – EYE MOVEMENT DESENSITIZATION AND REPROCESSING THERAPY. 2017. Accessed March 11, 2017. http://www.emdr.com/what-is-emdr/.

10 Howard, Sethanne, and Mark W. Crandall, MD. "Post Traumatic Stress Disorder What Happens in the Brain?" January 1, 2007. Accessed September 30, 2014. http://www.washacadsci.org/Journal/Journalarticles/V.93-3-Post Traumatic Stress Disorder. Sethanne Howard and Mark Crandalll.pdf.

11 Whittemore, Brain Injury Hope Foundation, Laura L., and Mary Ann Keatley, PhD, CCC. "BrainLine Military: Recovering from Mild Traumatic Brain Injury." Recovering from Mild Traumatic Brain Injury. Accessed January 10, 2015. http://www.brainlinemilitary.org/content/2009/11/recovering-from-mild-traumatic-brain-injury_pageall.html.

12 Gaultiere, Bill. "Calm Your Anxious Mind." Soul Shepherding. July 13, 2016. Accessed March 12, 2017. http://www.soulshepherding.org/2002/08/calm-your-anxious-mind/.

13 Ibid.

14 Ibid.

15 Ibid.

16 A SAMHSA Publication: Substance Abuse and Mental Health Services Administration, University of New Hampshire. "Dealing with the Effects of Trauma – A Self Help Guide." Counseling Center. August 14, 2012. Accessed March 13, 2015. http://unhcc.unh.edu/dealing-effects-trauma---self-help-guide.

Thrive With Hope

Online Community

IF YOU HAVE BEEN THROUGH a catastrophic event, visit www. ThriveWithHope.com for resources and encouragement.

Each year, millions of people are affected by natural disasters. Nearly everyone is affected by personal trauma at some point in their lives.

The psychological and physiological effects of these events, such as depression, anxiety, and stress, can be debilitating. No matter what challenges people encounter, they can recover.

Shauna's journey resulted in authoring *Fire of Hope* and founding the Thrive With Hope community.

An important part of recovery is strong support. Thrive With Hope provides a safe place for you to:

- Connect with others who understand trauma
- Find resources to begin your healing journey
- Get help moving from being a survivor to a thriver
- Flourish after a devastating event

Continue your journey today by visiting the
Thrive With Hope community.
www.ThriveWithHope.com
Facebook.com/ShaunaHoeyAuthor

Photo by Andrea Edwards

About Shauna L. Hoey

SHAUNA L. HOEY is a veteran educator who has developed curricula, workshops, and led support groups over the past twenty-five years. After her devastating experience in the Waldo Canyon fire, Shauna created trauma recovery tools, founded ThriveWithHope.com, a web-based community, and wrote *Fire of Hope* to help others find their way back to wholeness, too.

Shauna is married to her best friend, Rex. Their blended family of six amazing children and three grandchildren fill them with love beyond measure. They live in Manitou Springs, Colorado with their two youngest children and their Cavalier King Charles Spaniels.

CPSIA information can be obtained
at www.ICGtesting.com
Printed in the USA
FFHW01n0009240918
48535922-52421FF